THE FIRST WORLD WAR

Barry Bates

GENERAL EDITOR Jon Nichol

Contents

SIMON & SCHUSTER
EDUCATION

THE HISTORY PROJECT
(Formerly *Blackwell History Project*)

To Debra

© Barry Bates 1984

First published in 1984 by
Basil Blackwell Ltd
Reprinted 1986, 1987 (twice), 1989, 1991

Reprinted in 1992, 1993 by
Simon & Schuster Education

Simon & Schuster Education
Campus 400
Maylands Avenue
Hemel Hempstead
Herts HP2 7EZ

ISBN 0 7501 0434 1

Designed by Sue Richards
Printed in Hong Kong by Wing King Tong Co. Ltd.

Acknowledgements

BBC Hulton Picture Library 3(A) (E), 11(F), 33(E), 40(B); British
Library 12(B), 20(C), 28(B), 41(J); Camera Press: Cover; Centre
for the Study of Cartoons and Caricature, The University of Kent
at Canterbury 45(D); Commonwealth War Graves Commission
48(A); Culver Pictures, Inc. 31(H) (J); Mary Evans Picture Library
39(H); Imperial War Museum 4(F), 8(C), 13(G), 15(F), 16(B) (C),
17(H), 18(E), 20(D), 21(H) (J), 22(A), 23(D), 26(C), 28(A), 29(E),
32(A), 33(G), 34(A) (F), 35(H) (J), 36(D) (E), 37(H), 38(C);
Mansell Collection 10(A), 18(C), 24(A) (D); Novosti Press
Agency 30(E), Popperfoto 9(D), 25(E), 27(E), 40(A), 48(B);
Punch Publications Ltd 44(B) (C); South-Western Examinations
Board 5(J); Topham Picture Library 11(E).

1 Sarajevo

A Archduke Franz Ferdinand of Austria and his wife, shortly before the assassination

E The arrest of the suspected gunman

The heir to the Austrian throne, Archduke Franz Ferdinand, arrived at Sarajevo on a Sunday morning in June 1914. Look at **A.** You can see he was in military uniform. He was going to inspect Austrian troops in the town. Sarajevo was the main town in Bosnia, a province of the Austro-Hungarian Empire. Many Serbs lived there and they wanted Bosnia to become part of Serbia. There was a Serbian terrorist group, the 'Black Hand', so it was a risky visit. **B** will tell you what Franz Ferdinand thought of the risks.

❝ I do not care one tiniest bit about this. I am Inspector General of the Austrian armed forces. I must go to Sarajevo. The soldiers would never be able to explain my absence. ❞ (**B**)

On the way to the town hall, a bomb was thrown. The man who threw it said later: 'I . . . noticed how Franz Ferdinand looked at me with a cold, stiff glare.' Franz Ferdinand knocked the bomb into the road. Twenty people were killed. When he arrived at the town hall, Franz Ferdinand was angry: **C** gives some of his comments.

❝ Mr Mayor, I come here on a visit and I get bombs thrown at me. It is outrageous ... General Potierek (Governor of Bosnia), what about these bombs? Will it happen again? (Potierek replied: Your Imperial Highness, you can travel quite happily. I take the responsibility.') ❞ (**C**)

He decided to cancel the rest of his tour. His route back to the station was changed for reasons of safety, but it seems that nobody told the driver. Read the account by Count Harrach:

❝ At Appel Quay, Potierek shouted at the driver 'Stop, you are going the wrong way'. As we reversed, there were shots. Her Highness was hit; she sank to her knees, her face between the archduke's feet. I thought she had fainted from shock. Franz Ferdinand, blood pouring from his lips, shouted 'Sopherl, Sopherl, don't die. Live for our children'. I seized him by the coat collar to stop his head sinking forward. 'Is your Highness in great pain?' I asked. He replied 'It is nothing'. His expression changed and six or seven more times . . . he repeated 'It is nothing', slowly losing consciousness and losing his voice. ❞ (**D**)

By 11.30 pm, the royal couple were dead. Photograph **E** shows the arrest of the suspected gunman. These murders led to a war in which millions of soldiers would die. The First World War would begin one month later.

?????????????????

1 Prepare an on-the-spot newspaper report of the assassination.

2 After the killing, the terrorists sent a telegram to Belgrade, capital of Serbia. It read: 'Excellent sale of horses'. What do you think it meant?

3 You meet the ghost of Franz Ferdinand. What does it tell you about what took place on the day of the killing?

4 What types of evidence can you find from this page which would be available to the historian who wished to make a study of the murder?

2 The Alliances

Austria wanted to take revenge on Serbia for the murders of Franz Ferdinand and his wife. But why did other countries become involved? To understand, we must go back to 1871.

In that year, the German Empire had been created after a war with France. Germany kept two areas of land, Alsace and Lorraine, which had belonged to France before the war. Because she feared France would try to get them back, Germany looked for strong friends. She was able to make *alliances* with Austria and Russia. This is part of the agreement with Austria in 1879:

❛ *Should, contrary to the hope and desire of the two contracting parties, one of the Empires be attacked by Russia, each promises to help the other. This treaty, to avoid misinterpretation, shall be kept secret.* ❜ (**A**)

Austria and Russia were to fall out. Germany remained as an ally of Austria, and Italy joined them to form the Triple Alliance. Russia was left without an ally until 1892. Source **B** shows which alliance she was able to make.

❛ *If France is attacked by Germany or by Italy supported by Germany, Russia shall use all her forces to attack Germany. If Russia is attacked by Germany or by Austria supported by Germany, France shall attack Germany. If the Triple Alliance powers begin to mobilize, France and Russia would move theirs as close as possible to the frontiers.* ❜ (**B**)

These alliances were meant to be defensive. They were supposed to work only if the enemy attacked first.

There were reasons why the countries might fall out with one another. Germany wanted to gain colonies in places like Africa, as other countries had done. A British Foreign Office official warns of this danger:

❛ *The dream of an Empire has taken a deep hold on the German imagination . . . all declare with one voice: We must have colonies and we must have a fleet . . . The colonies we are bound to acquire . . . a healthy country like Germany with its 60 million inhabitants must expand to have territories to which its overflowing inhabitants can emigrate. When told the world is now parcelled up, the reply is . . . The world belongs to the strong.* ❜ (**C**)

The German Kaiser, Wilhelm II, had admired the British Navy on visits to his royal relations in England. In 1900

F   The British battleship, *HMS Dreadnought*

G   The proposal for cuts in the Navy provoked strong protests

THE NAVY LEAGUE

THE NAVY PROTECTS YOUR FOOD
THE NAVY PROTECTS YOUR WAGES
THE NAVY INSURES PEACE
THE NAVY PREVENTS INVASION

MR BURROWS WANTS
TO CUT DOWN THE NAVY

The Navy League
urges you to put

THE NAVY FIRST
AND
BURROWS LAST.

J A cartoon showing the world alliances before the First World War

Germany began the build-up of a large navy. **D**, from the German Navy Law, gives some of the reasons:

> *To protect German trade and commerce, only one thing is enough – Germany must have a fleet ... it is not absolutely essential that the German fleet be as strong as that of the greatest naval power for a great naval power will not be in a position to concentrate all its forces against us. The defeat of the strong German navy would so weaken the enemy that in spite of the victory his own supremacy would no longer be assured by a fleet of sufficient strength.* (**D**)

After many years as a neutral power, Great Britain now felt challenged. Part of a speech by Winston Churchill gives one or two clues to the threat:

> *The purpose of the British navy is defensive. There is a difference between British naval power and that of the great and friendly German empire. Our empire is existence to us; it is expansion to them ... the whole fortunes of our race and empire would perish if our naval supremacy was impaired. It is our navy which makes Britain a great power. Germany was one before she had a ship.* (**E**)

In 1906, HMS *Dreadnought* (**F**) had been built to a new design which made older battleships out-of-date. But Germany was developing new ships of her own. There were demands in Britain for more spending on defence, and the suggestion that cuts should be made in the Royal Navy met with an outcry (**G**).

Concerned at Germany's growing strength, Britain signed an alliance with Japan and was friendly with France and Russia. King Edward VII wrote to the Russian ambassador in London:

> *Since ... a solution has been found to the disputes which dragged on for years between England and France. I hope for a similar agreement with Russia. My new ambassador has instructions to work for cordial relations between us.* (**H**)

??????????????????

1 Look at cartoon **J**. Identify Britain, Germany, France, Italy, Russia, Austria and Japan. What point is the cartoonist trying to make?

2 Why is the reference to Russia in **A** surprising?

3 Examine all the evidence, imagine it is 1904, then write to the British prime minister advising whether he should make an alliance with Germany, or with Russia and France.

4 The various alliances have been described as 'two sets of mountaineers roped together'. What are the advantages and disadvantages of being roped together? What are the relationships today between the countries involved?

5 Explain in writing how the world came to be divided into two sets of alliances before 1914.

3 Two Trouble Spots

Morocco

Examine map **A**. It shows how European countries took over parts of Africa in the nineteenth century. By the turn of the century a tug of war had developed over Morocco. In 1906, Kaiser Wilhelm II made a speech in which he demanded that there should be a conference of the leading countries in Europe to discuss the future of Morocco. At the conference, held at Algeciras, only Austria accepted Germany's claim to Morocco. France was accepted as a 'policeman' for Morocco but slowly began to gain control over the country, and was obviously trying to make it a French colony.

In 1911, Germany sent a warship, the *Panther,* into the port of Agadir. **B** is a statement by a German Foreign Office official. Think of some reasons why it was sent.

❝ *In a quarter of an hour the bomb explodes. At twelve o'clock our ambassador will announce the arrival of the 'Panther' at Agadir. We have caused German firms and businessmen to send complaints. We chose Agadir because there are no French or Spanish there. It leads to Sus, the richest mineral and agricultural part of South Morocco. We shall take and keep this place.* ❞ (**B**)

If Germany gained control of Agadir, she would then threaten the French control of Morocco. This meant a major crisis among Europe's countries. **C** gives the French reaction:

❝ *France does not want war but she would not refuse it at the cost of her honour. Her mind is made up. If war were to break out it would be because we are attacked by an unscrupulous enemy who still believes force is sufficient excuse for his brutalities.* ❞ (**C**)

Britain showed that it would stand by France. Faced by the threat of war, Germany accepted that France was the supreme power in Morocco. In return, Germany received a piece of the Congo of much less worth than Morocco. The incident was soon over. A German politician remembers:

❝ *Like a damp squib it startled, then amused the world and ended by making us look ridiculous.* ❞ (**D**)

The Germans remained bitter over the part played by Britain. These words were spoken in the German parliament in November 1911:

❝ *Like a flash of lightning in the night these events have shown the German people where its enemy is . . . When it seeks a place in the sun, when it seeks the place allowed to it by destiny, where is the state which thinks it can decide this matter. When the hour comes we are ready for sacrifices of blood and treasure.* ❞ (**E**)

Do you think it is fair? After the incident, the alliances were strengthened as plans were worked out in case of war.

The Balkans

Think of the problems that arise because England, Wales, Scotland and Northern Ireland – four nations – are governed together. In the area known as the Balkans (map **F**), the Austrian Empire was made up of no less than eleven national groups. The Turkish (Ottoman) Empire was crumbling in the late nineteenth century and Austria watched anxiously as quarrels broke out. Austria and Russia were trying to expand into the Balkans.

In 1912, a Balkan war broke out. The great powers almost became involved as the local disagreements started to threaten them. A German ambassador in the region advised Austria:

A Africa, 1914

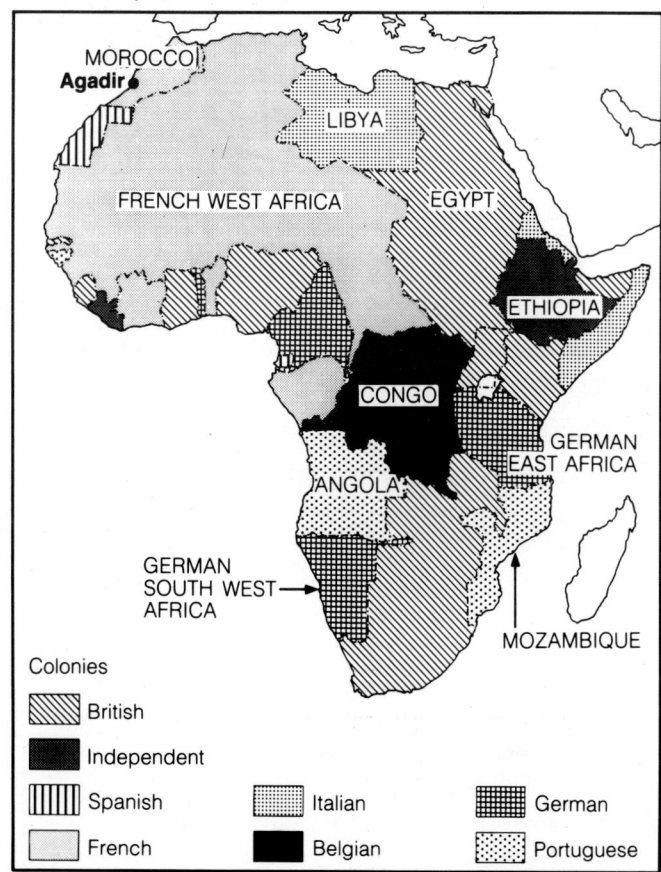

MOROCCO
Agadir
LIBYA
FRENCH WEST AFRICA
EGYPT
ETHIOPIA
CONGO
GERMAN EAST AFRICA
ANGOLA
GERMAN SOUTH WEST AFRICA
MOZAMBIQUE

Colonies

▨ British

■ Independent

▥ Spanish

▦ Italian

▧ German

☐ French

■ Belgian

▨ Portuguese

F The Balkans, 1878, showing the peoples and countries involved in the conflict

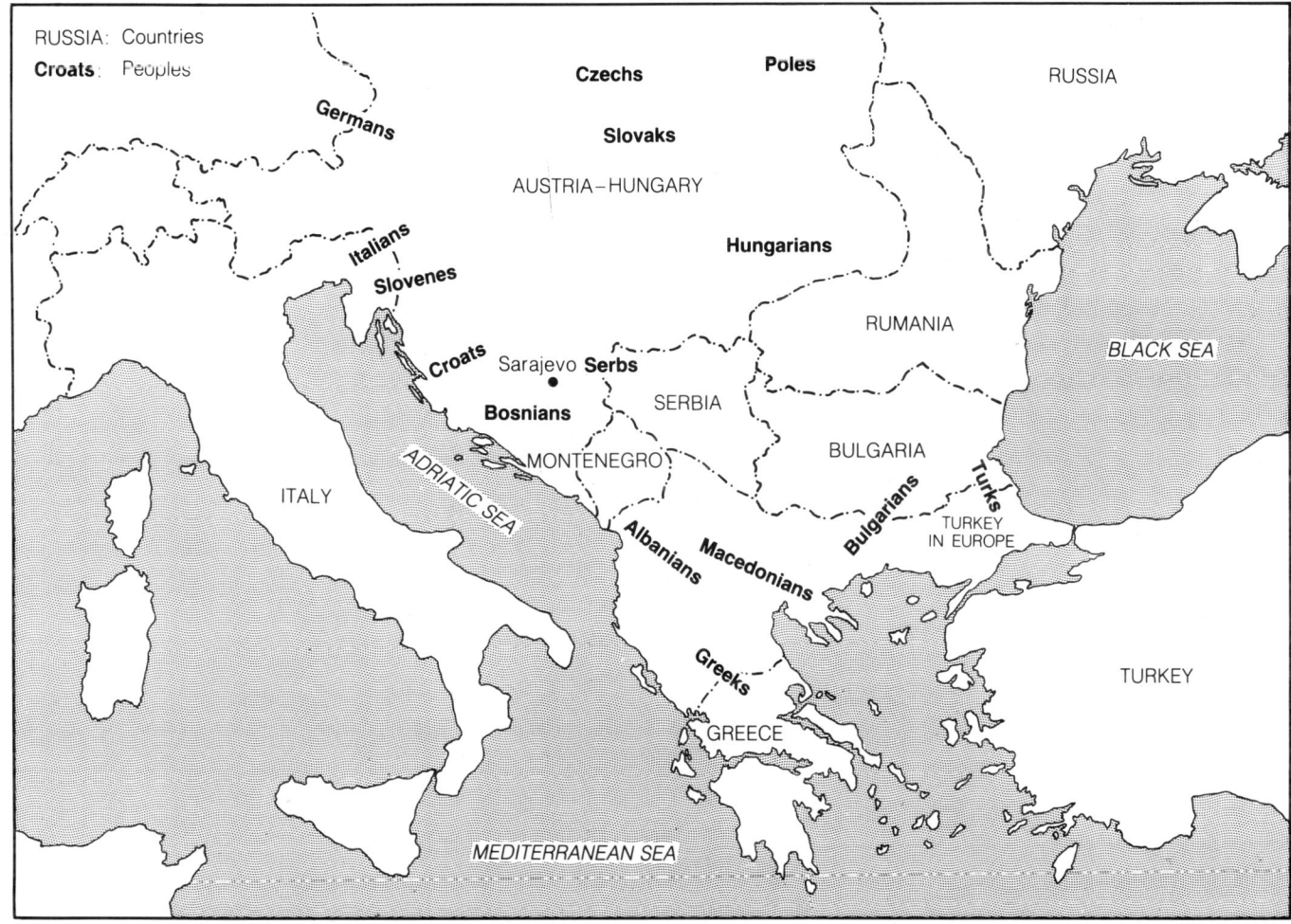

If the Austrian monarchy does not pull itself together there will be a defeat for the now dominant German race. The flood will then be impossible to contain in its banks. **(G)**

The great powers (Britain, Russia, Germany, Austria) tried to force peace on the small countries at a conference in London in 1913, but a new war broke out. This time, Rumania and Greece fought Bulgaria over the land they won from Turkey.

The confusion was finally sorted out in August 1913, but much bitterness remained. Serbia hated Austria, which had made sure that land gained during the war was taken away again. Serbia needed this land as it would give her seaports on the Adriatic Sea.

Russia had reasons for supporting Serbia. A Russian politician said:

This is perfect if only it could come off. Bulgaria and Serbia allied – 500 000 bayonets to guard the Balkans. This would bar the road forever to German penetration, Austrian invasion. **(H)**

By 1914, the Balkans had become a major trouble spot, rather like the Middle East is today. An incident might involve Austria and Russia, and the alliances would make sure that the rest of Europe was drawn in.

??????????????????

1 Compare map **A** with a modern map of Africa. What changes do you notice?

2 **a** Why did Russia support Serbia?
b Why did Austria want to prevent Serbia from having seaports on the Adriatic coast?

3 Why did countries want to gain colonies in the late nineteenth century? What do we think of such ideas today?

4 Make up a short conversation between a Frenchman and a German discussing the Agadir crisis a year after it happened. They should discuss who was to blame, why it nearly led to world war, and whether it was important to the countries concerned.

4   War Plans

The murder of Archduke Franz Ferdinand and his wife in the Balkans brought about a war which, for most of the Britons involved, was fought in northern France.

Each country had worked out war plans in advance. Those of France involved the use of precise railway timetables, with trains being in position to take units of soldiers wherever they were needed. A British soldier, who watched the French mobilization, described how rigid the plans were:

... every man has to know where he is to join (the army) and get there at a given time. Each unit, once complete and fully equipped, must be ready to proceed at a given day at the appointed hour to a prearranged place in a train ... which must move according to a prearranged railway timetable ... No change, no alteration is possible during mobilization. Improvisation (working things out as you go along) *when dealing with three million men and the movement of 4728 trains as the French had to do is out of the question.* (**A**)

The German war plan (**B**) had been drawn up in 1905, by General Schlieffen. His plan assumed that Germany

B   The Schlieffen Plan

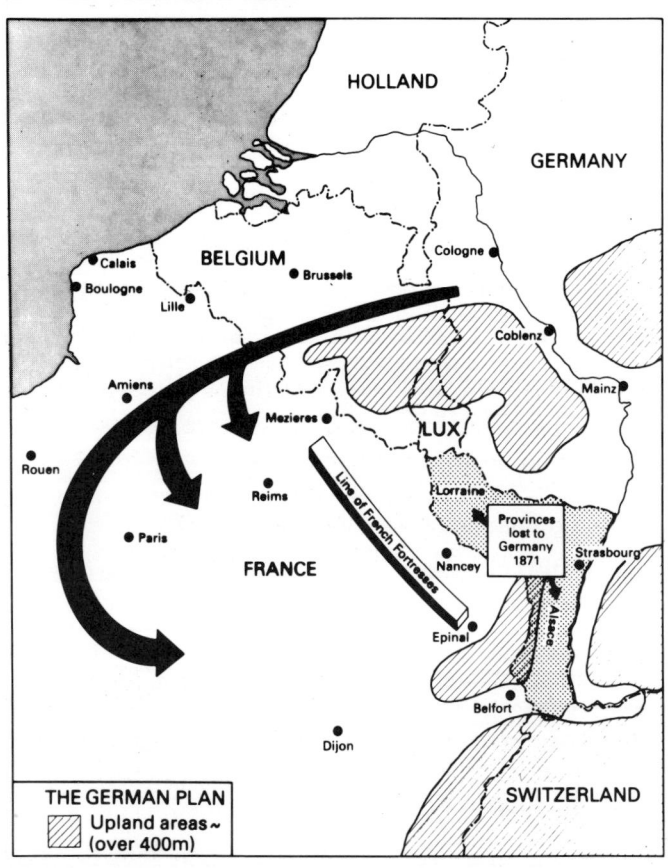

THE GERMAN PLAN
Upland areas ~ (over 400m)

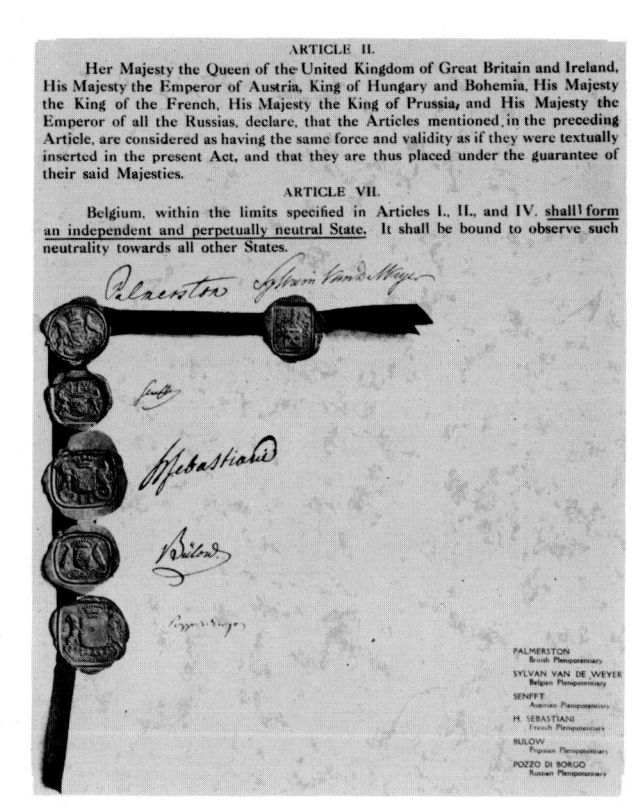

ARTICLE II.
Her Majesty the Queen of the United Kingdom of Great Britain and Ireland, His Majesty the Emperor of Austria, King of Hungary and Bohemia, His Majesty the King of the French, His Majesty the King of Prussia, and His Majesty the Emperor of all the Russias, declare, that the Articles mentioned in the preceding Article, are considered as having the same force and validity as if they were textually inserted in the present Act, and that they are thus placed under the guarantee of their said Majesties.

ARTICLE VII.
Belgium, within the limits specified in Articles I., II., and IV. shall form an independent and perpetually neutral State. It shall be bound to observe such neutrality towards all other States.

PALMERSTON
British Plenipotentiary
SYLVAN VAN DE WEYER
Belgian Plenipotentiary
SENFFT
Austrian Plenipotentiary
H. SEBASTIANI
French Plenipotentiary
BÜLOW
Prussian Plenipotentiary
POZZO DI BORGO
Russian Plenipotentiary

C   A facsimile of the 1839 Treaty of London: the 'scrap of paper'

would face a war on two fronts – against Russia and France. To win such a war would be difficult. He proposed to hold back the Russian army, which he assumed would be slow to mobilize. The bulk of German forces would knock out France and then return to concentrate on Russia. The plan did not attack Russia first, in part because a knockout blow would be difficult to achieve (Compare Napoleon and Hitler's attempts). The countdown to war (page 10) shows how important the Schlieffen plan was in 1914 in starting the war. By looking carefully at the plan you can work out some of its likely defects.

Britain joins the war

Britain claimed that Belgium had been declared a neutral country by the Treaty of London in 1839 (**C**). On the basis of this 'scrap of paper', Britain gave an ultimatum to Germany: get out of Belgium or we will fight you.

The Germans took no notice, and many were surprised when Britain declared war. King George V was a cousin of Kaiser Wilhelm II of Germany (**D**). However, there was tension between Britain and Germany (page

6), and public opinion was strongly in favour of war. King George V wrote in his diaries:

❝ *Germany declared war on Russia this evening … Whether we shall be dragged into it God only knows … France is begging us to come to their help … I think it will be impossible to keep out (of the war) as we cannot allow France to be smashed.* ❞ (**E**)

Later, he recorded:

❝ *Now everyone is for war and helping our friends. Orders for mobilization of the army will be issued at once.* ❞

British cabinet minister Sir Edward Grey wrote:

❝ *I was myself stirred with resentment at … Germany's crime in precipitating the war, and all I knew of Prussian militarism was hateful. But these must not be our motives for going to war … The real reason (is) that if we didn't stand by France and stand up for Belgium against this aggression we should be isolated, discredited and hated.* ❞ (**F**)

The German chancellor (prime minister) was most upset. A report from the British ambassador explained how he felt:

D Royal cousins: King George V and Kaiser Wilhelm II

❝ *(The chancellor) said that the steps taken by His Majesty's Government were terrible to a degree just for one word, 'neutrality', a word in wartime so often disregarded. Just for a scrap of paper Great Britain was going to make war on a kindred nation who desired nothing more than friendship. He held Great Britain responsible for terrible events that might happen.* ❞ (**G**)

Sir Edward Grey, waiting for the midnight deadline when war would be declared, said:

❝ *The lamps are going out all over Europe. We shall not see them lit again in our time* ❞ (**H**)

???????????????????

1 Look at map **B**.
  a Why did Schlieffen not push his main attack through Alsace-Lorraine?
  b Why was the main attack to pass through Belgium?
  c Is the plan directed at a particular place? If so, what place?
  d What do the arrows tell about the plan's approach to Paris and the French army strongholds?
  e What did Germany expect France to do if the plan succeeded?
  f Could Germany have approached France from any other direction?

2 A makes it clear that mobilization must be smooth, with nothing left to chance. Why were armies anxious to mobilize first? Why, once started, is the movement to war so difficult to stop?

3 You are a German army officer. Write to your commanding officer, warning him about the defects of the Schlieffen plan.

4 a Which word best describes Grey's attitude to war: hopeful, aggressive, resentful, happy?
  b How could Britain prevent German forces from passing through the English Channel? (Grey said that we should not allow this.)
  c Did Germany sign 'the scrap of paper'?
  d Who, in Grey's opinion, was to be blamed for the outbreak of war?

5 It has been said that people in Europe in 1914 were so nationalistic that politicians could not have prevented war. What note in the king's diary reflects this?

6 E and **F** give a British viewpoint. Work out a German viewpoint attacking the British decision to enter the First World War.

9

5 Countdown to War

A Grey
British Foreign Secretary

Poincaré
French President

Bethmann-Hollweg
German Chancellor

Moltke
German Army Chief

Immediate reaction to the murder of Franz Ferdinand was one of shock. The Austrian Emperor, Franz Joseph, said that the murders were 'horrible' but believed that God was paying Franz Ferdinand back for having married Sophia who was not a member of royalty. Most newspapers expected Austria to use the murders as an excuse to attack Serbia. It took Austria about one month to do this, and the rest of Europe one week to join in.

Countdown

29 June 1914 Austria decides to use the murders as an excuse to deal with Serbia. She asks Germany for help in case of war.

6 July Germany sends her reply: we will stand by you.

❝ *His Majesty desires to say that he is not blind to the danger which threatens Austria-Hungary and thus the Triple Alliance as a result of Russian and Slav agitation.*

Finally as regards Serbia, His Majesty cannot of course interfere in the dispute now going on between Austria and that country. The Emperor Franz Joseph may rest assured that His Majesty will faithfully stand by Austria-Hungary as is required by the obligations of his alliances and ancient friendship. ❞ (**B**)

23 July Austria sends Serbia an ultimatum. It threatens war unless Serbia agrees to their demands. The most important of these is that Austrian officials should be allowed into Serbia to arrest those responsible for the murder.

24 July Russia decides she will help Serbia.

25 July Serbia replies to the ultimatum. She accepts most of the clauses but refuses to let Austria in. Russia prepares to mobilize.

28 July Austria declares war on Serbia.

29 July Russia mobilizes.

1 August 6pm: Germany declares war on Russia. Germany mobilizes. France mobilizes. Germany asks France how she will act. 'According to her interests' is the reply. Germany decides to use the Schlieffen plan. This means she will attack France first.

2 August Germany asks Belgium to allow the German army through into France. Belgium refuses.

3 August 6.45pm: Germany declares war on France.

4 August Germany invades Belgium. Britain sends Germany an ultimatum asking her to withdraw from Belgium. No reply is received and by midnight Britain and Germany are at war.

Use **C** to work out whether Germany expected a full-scale war:

❝ *Austria has resolved to march into Serbia. His Majesty (Kaiser Wilhelm II) and the Foreign and War Ministry approve of this decision and will cover Austria if Russia helps Serbia. But His Majesty does not think Russia will intervene ... and has decided to go on his northern holiday cruise as planned.* ❞ (**C**)

D Germany mobilizes: Berlin, August 1914

E Enthusiastic crowds outside a recruitment meeting in London

The alliances had held and the First World War – the Great War, as it came to be known – had begun. Photographs **D** and **E** show how the public reacted to the news in Berlin and London.

??????????????????

1 a Which of the great powers did not support its alliance and go to war in 1914?
b What fact from **C** supports the idea that Germany did not expect a full-scale war?

2 Why did . . .
a Austria wish to attack Serbia?
b Austria need German support?
c Russia wish to help Serbia?
d Germany support Austria?
e Germany attack France?
f Britain declare war on Germany?
(You will need to look at evidence in previous chapters.)

3 How would you have set about making peace in July and August 1914?

4 Using evidence in the book so far, explain how war broke out in 1914. Include the following factors: immediate causes, nationalism, colonial rivalry, the alliances, the arms race.

6 The Western Front 1914-17

'It will be over by Christmas.' That's what some people thought when war broke out. The Schlieffen plan did not go well. The Belgians fought bravely and Brussels did not fall till 20 August. By then, Germany was worried at the speed with which the Russians had got their armies together, so some troops had to be sent to the Eastern Front. 125,000 soldiers of the British Expeditionary Force were sent over to help the French, but **A** shows that the Germans did not expect much opposition from them. The Kaiser told his troops:

❝ *It is my royal command that you concentrate all your energies . . . on one purpose, that is . . . to exterminate first the treacherous English.* ❞ **(A)**

The German commander decided not to divide his armies by encircling Paris, but to make a mass attack on the city. The series of attacks between 6-13 September are known as the Battle of the Marne. The French used all available transport to move men to the front and the German advance was stopped after a week. The German chief of staff told the Kaiser. 'Your Majesty, we have lost the war'.

By the end of 1914 bitterness between the two sides increased. **B** gives some clues as to why the Allies disliked Germany.

The line of battle (map **C**) changed little until the end of the war. Each side tried to break through, to gain land and advantage.

In 1916, both sides prepared for a new mass attack. The Germans chose the old fortress of Verdun. You can work

C The Western Front, 1915-17

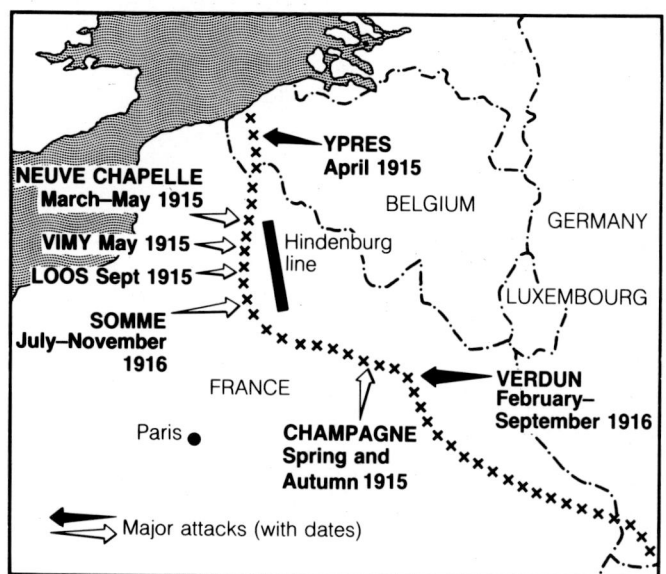

out from the map why it was an obvious target. A Swiss observer of the battle wrote:

❝ *The battle is now at its fiercest phase. But what will have been gained even if the French or the Germans manage to break through? I guess that the Germans have pushed 800 000 men into Verdun. By now they must have lost 300 000 killed, wounded or taken prisoner. Why do they go on? The explanation I've heard makes little sense. They are trying to tire out the enemy. What a mistake – you lose more men attacking than defending.* ❞ **(D)**

B Allegations of German atrocities in the British press

Page 2.—DAILY SKETCH.   SATURDAY, JANUARY 9, 1915.

CAN YOU STILL HANG BACK? IT MAY BE YOUR SISTER NEXT

GERMANY'S BLACK PAGE OF SHAME.

Slaughter, Outrage, Pillage And Arson Shown In Official Report.

NEITHER SEX NOR AGE SPARED.

The Bavarians' Ferocity Against Hapless Civilians.

3,000 BELGIANS KILLED.

A terrible record of slaughter and outrage by the German troops in Northern France is revealed in an official report issued by the French Government yesterday—a black page in German history only equalled by that of their atrocities in Belgium.

Foremost among the troops who thus disgraced their name were the Bavarians, whose King in his birthday message issued this week talks of their ancient glory and renown and of their cultural development.

The Commission of Inquiry into German atrocities in Belgium has also terminated its labours so far as they concern the Province of Namur.   The results of the

THE BAVARIANS' CULTURAL DEVELOPMENT.

Every German is now imbued with only one thought, joyfully to make every sacrifice for the honour and protection of the Fatherland.

With pride and joy I look upon the brave Bavarian army, which has confirmed its ancient renown and in glorious battles has proved itself a worthy member of the German army.

My confidence is immutable that the overwhelming defeat of our enemies will assure lasting peace, which is worth heavy sacrifices, and enable me to lead my people forward on the road to economical and cultural development.   God protect beloved Bavaria.—Birthday message of King Ludwig of Bavaria to his people.

The greater part of the deviltry in the Vosges seems to have been the work of Bavarians.

At Gerbeviller they proceeded to avenge their losses on the civil population.   They burst into the houses, shooting, stabbing, and capturing the inhabitants—sparing neither age nor sex—and burning and sacking the houses.

A woman aged 78 was shot and her body afterwards shamefully profaned.

A man named Lingenheld was shot, and while he was still living the Bavarians poured petrol over him and set fire to it in the presence of his mother.—Extracts from the French official report on German atrocities.

PRIESTS TORTURED.

Revolting Cruelty To The Catholic Clergy In Belgium.

SACRILEGE AND MURDER.

Churches As Stables, Cures Flogged And Shot, And Bishops Ill-used.

The arrest of Cardinal Mercier appears to be but the climax to a policy of methodical maltreatment of the Catholic clergy of Belgium pursued by the German invaders from the first.

At the request of the Belgian Legation in London the Press Bureau yesterday issued a list of specific instances of barbarous ill-treatment, of which evidence has been collected by the commission of inquiry.

Not only have churches and religious houses been destroyed or profaned in almost every village and in many towns through which the German Army passed, but in many places the sacred vessels were stolen when they had not previously been placed in safe concealment. Churches and religious buildings have even been utilised as stables or prisons.

HOISTED ON A CANNON.

There is, in particular, the case of the aged priest of Buechen, Father M. de Clerck, who on August 21 was arrested by German soldiers

THESE MEN ARE "MAINTAINING THEIR ANCIENT GLORY"!

G   The battlefield at Ypres, 1917

The French fought hard, and as **E** shows, Germany lost many men in this futile attack.

The British attack, organised by General Haig, took place at the Somme. On the first day, 57 000 men were hit, of whom 20 000 died. A British artillery officer wrote:

❛ *1 July, Z Day. A lovely day. We opened a bombardment at 5 a.m. The assault took place at 7.30 a.m. 7.35, message from the Major. We've taken the front line with a casualty. 4th Division walked across! Shortly afterwards we changed our range from 5000 to 3000 yards which was a bit of a shock. They made a counter-attack and . . . our men were held up by the villages and enemy machine guns. Colossal casualties. We are all very depressed.* ❜ (**E**)

The cost of the Battle of the Somme was high:

❛ *The joint British-French attack was designed to relieve pressure on Verdun. The amount of land captured was about seven miles square. For this miserable fraction of the world's surface about three-quarters of a million British and French soldiers became casualties. The battle lasted between 1 July and 20 November 1916. British loss was 22 293 officers, 476 553 NCO's.* ❜ (**F**)

There had been no breakthrough by 1917. The British captured Messines Hill near Ypres (**G**), using one million tons of explosives. The roar could be heard in London, over one hundred miles away. Men close at hand lost their hearing. In 1917, Haig attacked the Germans at Passchendaele, hoping to capture the Belgian coast and stop German U-boats using its ports. The attack failed in the mud. 'Good God, did we really send men to fight in that', said Haig's chief of staff when he finally visited the scene.

Tanks were used on a large scale for the first time at Cambrai in November 1917. Before then, it was men and horses. **H** is an account by an airman who watched an attack:

❛ *There was I, in my ultra modern plane, while nearby men were on the oldest transport of all. The cavalry could not penetrate enemy lines thru' the barbed wire. Brave and beautiful horses struggled desperately to get through. Riders and mounts were sitting ducks for the enemy and many were shot down in the mud and wire.* ❜ (**H**)

J   Major battles 1915-17

	Place	Attacking force	Result
Jan/Mar 1915	Champagne	French	Small gains. No major breakthrough
Mar/May 1915	Neuve Chapelle	British	No breakthrough
April 1915	Ypres	German	Initial breakthrough soon stopped
May 1915	Vimy	French	Some small gains No breakthrough
Sept 1915	Loos	British	No breakthrough
Sept 1915	Champagne	French	Initial advance soon stopped
Feb/Sept 1916	Verdun	German	Massive casualties Fails to take the town
July/Nov 1916	Somme	British	Massive casualties Attack fails
Spring 1917	Champagne	French	No success, some French troops mutiny
June 1917	Messines Hill	British	Hill taken
Aug/Oct 1917	Passchendaele	British	Fails to free the Belgian coast

??????????????????

1 a Look at photograph **G**. Describe what is shown at 1, 2 and 3.
   b Find allegations of German atrocities in **B**. Then, from the German point of view, say why you think some of them might be lies.

2 What sentence in this chapter suggests that some generals and high-ranking officers did not realise the conditions in which the soldiers were fighting? What else suggests that the generals were remote from the fighting?

3 Imagine that you are the German chief of staff at the end of 1914. Explain to the Kaiser why you think the Schlieffen plan has failed, and why you thought the war was lost.

4 What evidence does **J** give of advance and progress by either side between 1915 and 1917?

7 Trench warfare: Deadlock

A Cross-section of trench

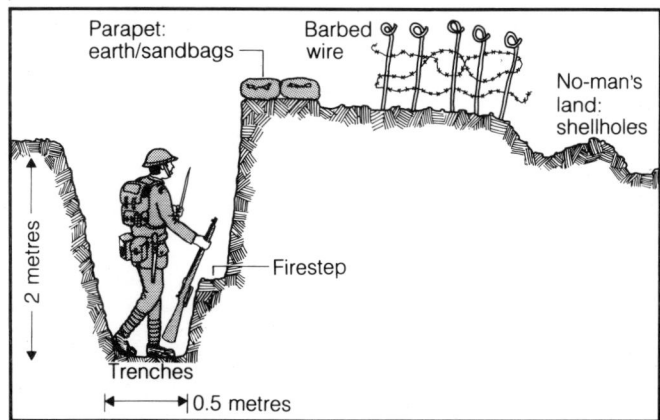

Autumn 1914. Both sides began to dig trenches to protect their armies during the winter, as it was risky to fight a pitched battle in the open. The generals thought that in the spring open warfare would begin again. They were wrong, for once the line of trenches was dug it proved hard for an army to break through. All attempts meant huge numbers of dead and wounded soldiers.

A is a cross-section of a trench, and **B** a plan of a typical trench system. German trenches were well built and planned.

A British soldiers tells us about them:

❝ *What was superior beyond doubt was the enemy trench system, built in thorough German fashion to a proper standard of strength and defended with large numbers of machine guns. The morale of the German troops was bound to be high as there was every likelihood they would beat off an attack . . . our trench warfare seemed based on the concept that we would not be stopping for long. The result was that we lived in . . . lousy scratch holes.* ❞
(**C**)   G. Coppard *With a Machine Gun to Cambrai*

To make advances, it was necessary to break through the other side's trench system. The British generals followed this plan:

1 Guns behind the front line bombard the enemy trenches. The shells are aimed to smash enemy trenches and rip holes in the barbed wire.
2 The men would climb out of their trenches and head for the enemy line. They carried rifles with fixed bayonets.
3 The troops hoped to overpower the enemy and capture their trenches.

Changes in tactics after 1914:
4 Poisonous gas was released against the enemy.
5 Tanks and aircraft would attack the enemy. Tanks could break through the trench system.

Two soldiers – one from each side – describe trench warfare:

❝ *Only the officers knew of the attack, the men not being told until just beforehand. At 4 p.m. the gas went off. The Germans stayed silent. The brigadier decided not to take too much for granted. After the bombardment he sent out an officer and twenty-five men as a feeling patrol. As the patrol reached the German wire there was a burst of machine gun and rifle fire. Only two men regained the trench . . . The Sergeant Major said, 'It's murder, Sir'. 'Of course it's murder, you bloody fool,' I agreed, 'but there's nothing else for it, is there?'* ❞ (**D**)
(**British**)   R. Graves *Goodbye to all that*

❝ *The bombardment stops. The attack has come . . . We use machine guns, rifles and hand grenades. The enemy cannot do much before they are within forty yards. A whole line has gone down before our machine guns. We retreat – leaving bombs behind us – the attack is crushed by our artillery . . . we arrive once more at our shattered*

B Plan of trench system

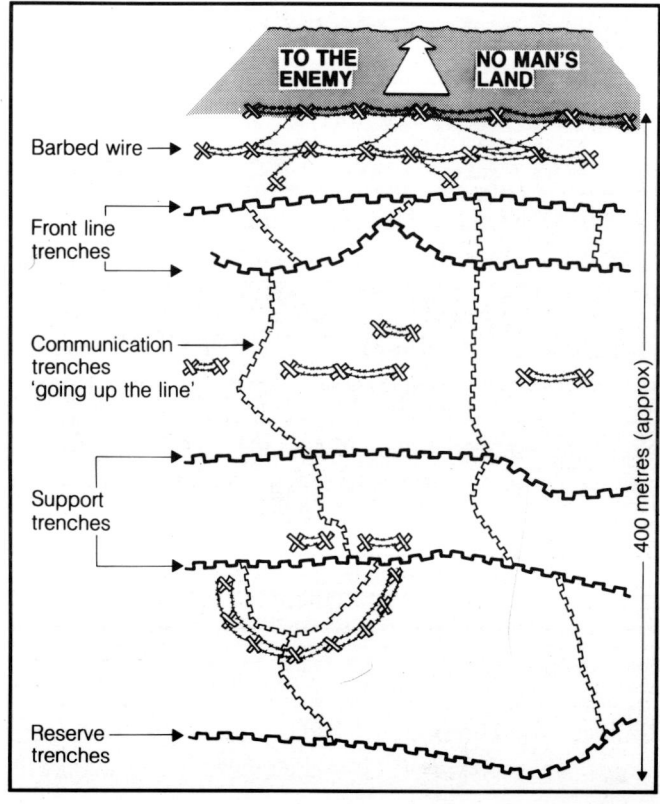

14

*trench, exhausted, without will. We kill because if we
don't destroy them they will destroy us. We go on to their
trench and bag five tins of corned beef. Occasionally
raids have been arranged to get it because we have
constant hunger.* **)** (**E**)

(**German**)   E.M. Remarque *All Quiet on the Western Front*

The area between the trenches was pounded by explod-
ing shells before the men 'went over the top'. Everything
was destroyed, and the area was called 'no man's land'.
Deep shell holes provided shelter for the men, but were
themselves a source of danger when filled with mud and
water (**F**).

A line of trenches stretched almost continuously
across Western Europe (map **G**) and altered little during
the four years of war. Compare the line of trenches with
the Western Front (map **C**, previous chapter).

Heavy guns caused most damage to the men in the
trenches, with machine gun fire second. There were
relatively few wounds from bayonets:

H Causes of wounds to British troops

> shell/trench mortar — 58 per cent
> rifle/machine gun — 39 per cent
> bombs/grenades — 2.9 per cent
> bayonet — 0.32 per cent

The historian A.J.P. Taylor suggests why neither side
could have broken through:

*The generals relied on mass, sheer weight of men. The
new recruits were trained to believe that bayonets were
the decisive weapon. As always happened defence moved
in men faster by rail than the attacks could move forward
by foot.* **)** (**J**)

F   After the Battle of Passchendaele: a derelict tank lies
stranded in a mud-filled shell crater

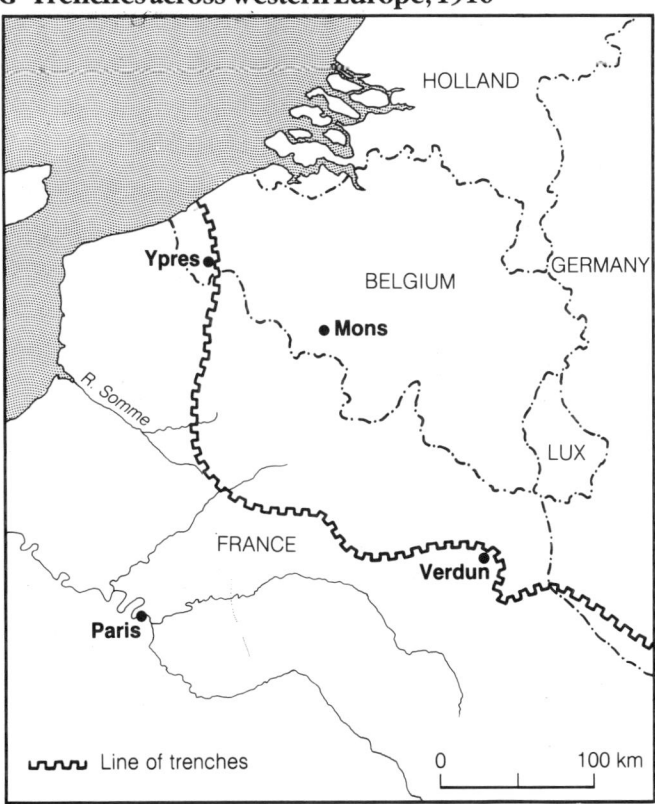

G Trenches across Western Europe, 1916

HOLLAND

Ypres

BELGIUM

GERMANY

Mons

R. Somme

LUX

FRANCE

Verdun

Paris

〰〰〰 Line of trenches   0   100 km

???????????????????

1 Look at **A**. What was the use of the firestep? the
parapet? the barbed wire?

2 If you were in charge of trench system **B,** how would
you defend it against the plan of attack as described
in points 1-5? Mention the artillery attack, the charge
of the enemy footsoldiers, your use of machine guns.

3 Look again at **B**. Why were there three main lines of
trenches? Why were the trenches zig-zagged? Why
was barbed wire set up in those places?

4 Imagine you are a soldier in the trenches. An attack
is just over. Many of your friends are hurt or dead.
Write a diary account of what happened. Mention the
bombardment, the charge, machine guns, hand to
hand fighting, death and wounds, smells, sounds,
your feelings.

5 Say how each of these led to deadlock on the
Western Front: defensive weapons such as barbed
wire and machine guns; the state of no man's land; the
way in which the troops attacked, and their weapons.

6 Suggest why the trench system shown on map **G**
lasted for so long.

7 Do figures support the idea that the bayonet was a
decisive weapon in the First World War?

8 Life in the Trenches

C British troops queue for dinner rations at mobile field kitchens

Many of the soldiers who served in the trenches in the First World War were not much older than people in a modern sixth form. None had experienced anything like it before, and a large number of men kept diaries or accounts of their life at the front. Some of the accounts have been made into books and films which, with the first-hand memories of survivors, tell us about conditions on the Western Front.

There was constant danger from attack by bombardments of heavy shelling, from snipers and mustard gas. A nurse behind the lines wrote of the effect of the gas:

❛ We have heaps of gassed cases. I wish those who call this a holy war could see the poor things burnt and blistered all over with great mustard-coloured, suppurating blisters, with blind eyes all sticky and glued together, always fighting for breath with voices a mere whisper saying their throats are closing and they will choke. ❜ **(A)**
(British) G. Chapman, *Vain Glory*

Hot food was difficult to prepare near the front line. Water was often short. The standard rations were corned beef ('bully beef') and hard biscuits. A soldier remembered:

❛ Many times we had only one slice of bread for breakfast and biscuits for tea. These were so hard you had to smash them with a stone. ❜ **(B)**

Food was issued from field kitchens (**C**) which were brought as close to the front as possible. Rum was often issued before the men took part in an attack.

Accommodation was in dugouts, which were holes made in the sides of trenches and covered with tarpaulin sheets. Wood, sandbags and any other materials that were available were used for building shelters (**D**). There was no comfort. Clothes and bodies became dirty because of the lack of washing facilities, and lice were a menace. They lived in hair and clothing and caused itching and irritation as they bit the skin. The men had various ways of dealing with them, but never managed to be free of them. A German soldier wrote:

❛ Killing each separate louse is hard work when a man has hundreds; they are hard to crack with one's fingernails. (One of my mates) has hung a boot polish tin over a lighted candle. We throw them in, crack, they are done for. ❜ **(E)**
(German) E.M. Remarque, *All Quiet on the Western Front*

In winter, deep mud was everywhere, and great numbers of rats lived off empty bully beef tins and dead bodies. It was not possible to bring back all the dead and wounded:

❛ We are able to bring in the wounded who do not lie too far off. But many have long to wait and we listen to them dying. For one we search for two days in vain. Kat thinks

D Soldiers resting in a front-line trench

he is hurt in the spine or pelvis – his chest cannot be injured otherwise he would not cry out. We crawl out at night but cannot find him. The first day he cries for help, next day he is delirious and cries for his family. In the morning we suppose he has gone to his rest. The dead lie unburied. We cannot bring them all in. If we did we should not know what to do with them. ❜ (**F**)

(**German**)   E.M. Remarque, *All Quiet on the Western Front*

Poor living conditions gave rise to health problems apart from wounds caused by gunfire and gas. The noise of the heavy guns was go great that many men suffered from some degree of deafness. A nervous condition called 'shellshock' was common, caused by living in an almost permanent state of tension. The result was a trembling of the limbs or the whole body, and stammering. Many soldiers realised that the experience of war would change them completely. One wrote:

❛ *... if we go back home we will be broken, worn out, rootless, without hope. Men will not understand us* ❜ (**G**)

On Christmas Day 1914, the first of the war, some troops from both sides made an unofficial peace. A football match was played, presents were exchanged and carols sung. The men were forbidden to let it happen again, and it did not. As the war dragged on, bitterness between the two sides increased to a point where accounts like this could be written:

❛ *On Christmas Eve we were told not to fraternize with the Germans. For my friends and myself we were in no mood for any joviality with Jerry. Since Loos we hated his bloody guts. Christmas Day: no parcels, no letters. Soggy rations – plus a few raisins covered in hairs from inside a sandbag. That night we saw some Jerries laying wire ... Snowy and I took a Vickers (machine gun) ... a hail of bullets and the ghostlike figures fell. The ground was raked to finish off any who were feigning death. Goodwill to all men meant nothing to us then.* ❜ (**H**)

(**British**)   G. Coppard, *With a Machine Gun to Cambrai*

The men knew that many of those who left the trenches in an attack (**J**) would be killed or wounded. They had to live with the sights and sounds of death:

❛ *9 June   Going along whistling I saw a group of men bending over a man lying in the bottom of a trench. He was making a snoring noise mixed with animal groans. At my feet lay his cap splashed with his brains. One can joke with a wounded man, one can disregard a dead man, but no one can joke over a man who takes three hours to die after the top of his head has been taken off by a bullet fired at twenty yards range.* ❜ (**K**)

(**British**)   Robert Graves, *Goodbye to all that*

J   Going 'over the top'

Some managed to take a lighthearted attitude, gambling with their lives:

❛ *Kendle and I were having great fun together. 'I'll have a shot at him again', he said as the helmet bobbed up again. I remember seeing him push his tin hat back from his forehead and raise himself before taking aim. After firing once he looked at us with a lively smile; a second later he fell sideways, a blotchy mark showed where the bullet had hit him above the eyes.* ❜ (**L**)

(**British**)   Siegfried Sassoon, *Memoirs of an Infantry Officer*

???????????????????

1 Imagine that you are one of the soldiers in photograph **D** who is writing. What story might he be telling?

2 What does the fraternization (friendly meeting) at Christmas 1914 tell you about the attitude of the men on both sides? Why do you think that it was forbidden?

3 Which piece of evidence shows a hardening of attitude towards the enemy?

4 What did the soldier mean when he wrote that he and his comrades would return home rootless, without hope, and misunderstood? What part of the short account shows that he did not feel sure that he would return home?

9 War at Sea

'For thirty years I have waited for this day,' said Admiral Beatty, commander of the Royal Navy, when war broke out in 1914. The war at sea did not start immediately because the main part of the German navy withdrew to port. This allowed the British to clear the seas of enemy ships that remained, and in 1915 there were no German surface ships left outside the ports and harbours. British ships blockaded the German ports, stopping all merchant ships and thus preventing supplies of food and goods from reaching Germany.

The German plan seemed to be to keep the British navy at sea. Occasionally, the German navy left port to attack British ships and to bombard towns within reach of their long-range guns (map **A**). Both sides scattered mines. A sailor on HMS *Tiger* wrote an account of a chase:

❛ *The news that they bombarded Great Yarmouth angered us. We steamed all night and arrived off Dogger Bank. The German admiral . . . was trying to lure us on to a German minefield. They headed for home, but soon we could see their topmasts on the horizon. We were gaining on them. Beatty wanted to 'sink the lot' but Admiral Moore confused his signals and we lost time. We finished off 'Blucher' . . . but we could go no further because they reached their own minefields. Beatty's ship, the 'Lion' was a dead duck.* ❜ (**B**)

A War in the North Sea

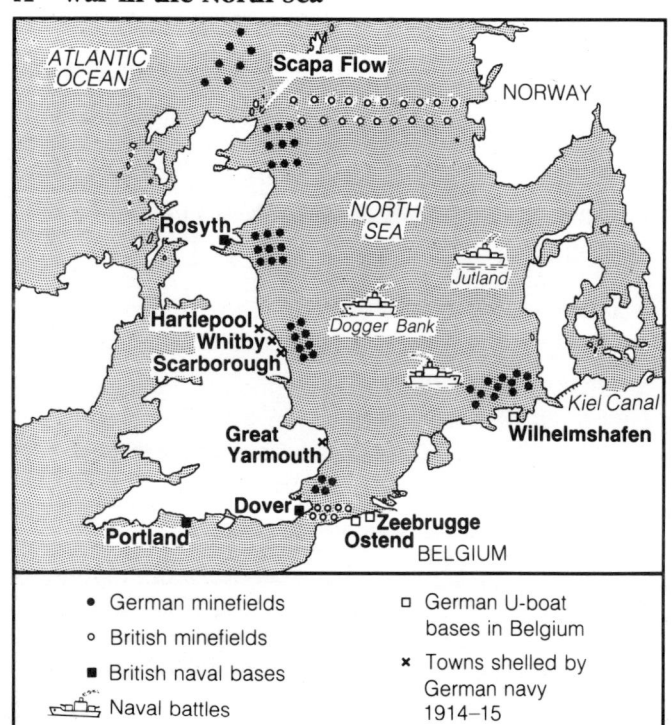

- • German minefields
- ○ British minefields
- ■ British naval bases
- 🚢 Naval battles
- ☐ German U-boat bases in Belgium
- × Towns shelled by German navy 1914–15

C A German U-boat

As the war went on, Germany built large numbers of submarines known as U-boats – *Unterseebooten* (**C**). Admiral Tirpitz realised that they were a deadly weapon against an island, as Britain was. They could stalk ships unseen, torpedo them and stop vital food, oil and raw materials from getting through. Britain, needing a great deal of imported food, would be starved into surrender.

Using Zeebrugge and Ostend in Belgium as bases, the German U-boats began to sink British ships. A sailor wrote:

❛ *The U-boat threat was always with us. The man up in the crow's nest had a cold, lonely job. He looked for the telltale puff of smoke on the horizon or for the wake of a torpedo, but in foggy weather we had to be alert. We would steer zigzag to make it hard for the U-boat to line up the periscope.* ❜ (**D**)

It became necessary to form British merchant ships into convoys (**E**) and escort them with naval vessels as a protection against U-boats. When America entered the war in 1917, their ships would escort British ships part-way across the Atlantic.

Anti-submarine devices were built. A depth charge containing 250 kilograms of explosive, timed to go off at a set depth, could be thrown about 150 metres. Listening aids were developed, so that the noise of a U-boat's engines would give away her position. Mines were improved, and many U-boats were destroyed by them.

In May 1915, U-20 torpedoed and sank the liner *Lusitania* en route from New York to Liverpool with 2150 passengers. There was a great public outcry at the news (**F**), but the Germans justified their action. An official communication from Berlin said:

❛ *The 'Lusitania' was naturally armed with guns as were most English steamers. Moreover it is well known here that she had large quantities of war material in her cargo. Her owners knew to what dangers the passengers were exposed. They alone bear all responsibility for what has happened.* ❜ (**G**)

E A British convoy steering a zig-zag course in a danger zone

One side supported the view that innocent people had died as a result of a cowardly act; the other side claimed that the *Lusitania* was carrying war materials. Over sixty years after the sinking, the *Sunday Times* of 15 August 1982 published this:

❛ *The 'Lusitania' was built for Cunard in 1906, financed by a massive government subsidy. Cunard in return agreed to build her so she could be converted into an armed cruiser . . . She had special mountings built into her decks which could take six-inch guns. There is no*

F The public outcry at the sinking of the *Lusitania*

WONDERFUL HEROISM IN THE LUSITANIA.

MOVING STORIES OF THE DISASTER.

HUNS' 1,447 VICTIMS.

AMERICAN WRATH WITH AUTHORS OF THE GREATEST CRIME.

IMPUDENT GERMAN FICTION.

The full narrative of the loss of the Lusitania accentuates the horror and wickedness o f the crome perpetrated by the German submarines. Babies and women have perished by the score; hundreds of peaceful noncombatants have been drowned to make a German holiday. The total number of saved is only 703 out of 2,150 souls on board.

The news of this dastardly outrage has been received with loathing and execration by civilised men. In Holland, in Italy, in Norway there is outspoken condemnation of its cowardly authors. In the United States intense indignation has been caused by this barbarous murder of American citizens. President Wilson's Government has asked Berlin to state whether Germany is responsible for it and to give full details. The President maintains the strictest reserve as to his attitude.

Germans are rejoicing with the high glee of fields over their infamy. Admiral von Tirpitz, whose son is in a British

the explosion as terrific. Clouds of smoke, coal dust, and débris were shot into the air. Everything below the Grand Saloon, says one witness, was "blown to smithereens." A man near the wineroom saw an uprush of flame and fragments, and recoiled instinctively into the wineroom for shelter from the flying splinters. The boiler-rooms and stokeholds were torn open, and probably most of the gallant engineers and stokers in them were killed then and there at their posts.

"By God, they've done it!" was the remark of an American who had been discussing the Germans' chance of torpedoing the ship. There is some doubt whether only one or two torpedoes were fired. It is possible that two torpedoes were discharged simultaneously from the double tubes which the newest German submarines carry and that they struck simultaneously. It is also possible that two were fired at a slight interval of time. Most of the survivors believe there was only one great explosion, but in the agony and stress of such a catastrophe the human mind is fallible. Here and there witnesses are found who declare that a second torpedo struck the Lusitania about half a minute after the first.

WAILING OF THE CHILDREN.

available evidence that the guns were fitted. But the Germans believed they were hidden just below deck and could be brought out in a matter of minutes. (In the war) on almost every voyage she was stuffed with war materials. On her last voyage there is convincing evidence that apart from five million rounds of ammunition, she carried a large quantity of explosive. ❜ (**H**)

U-20 had already attacked and sunk two ships in the five days she had been active off the west coast of Ireland. The *Lusitania* had no escort. There were suspicions that the British government had allowed the liner to sail into danger in order to draw the United States of America into the war (most of the passengers were American).

The Germans were worried that America would enter the war after the *Lusitania* incident. The U-boat campaign was slowed down for a time but on 31 January 1917 Germany announced that she would sink on sight all ships approaching Great Britain. In March and April of that year, 600 ships were sunk; one in four ships leaving Britain did not return and soon there was only a month's supply of grain left. Germany felt sure Britain was near to defeat.

However, Britain survived. A major reason for this was the convoy system of protecting merchant ships. By this method, losses were cut to 1 per cent from 25 per cent.

Another reason for Britain's survival was that by late 1917, after the USA entered the war (see p. 30), the Allies were building ships faster than they could be sunk, and U-boats were being sunk faster than they could be built.

???????????????????

1 Why was it easy for U-boats to break through the British blockade at the beginning of the First World War? What measures were developed to control this?

2 Use the evidence to prepare your views on the following statements:
  a Germany was not to blame for sinking the *Lusitania*.
  b There is no doubt that the *Lusitania* was carrying explosives.
  c Lives were lost because of mistakes by Britain.

3 How useful and reliable would each of the following be as evidence for a historian writing about the sinking of the *Lusitania*.
  a The wreck
  b The logbooks of the *Lusitania* and the *U-20*
  c Newspaper reports

4 Explain how Britain survived and finally defeated the U-boats.

10 War at Home (1)

Look again at the pictures in section 5. It might seem that everyone was behind the war effort. Not everyone in Britain was convinced that it was right to fight. Some politicians were put under pressure. Lord Riddell wrote in his diary:

❛ *Lloyd George* (a Liberal politician who became prime minister in 1916) ... *was in a difficult position. Friends ... bombarded him with telegrams to say any Liberal who supported the war would never be allowed to join another Liberal government. Lloyd George said that Germany's action had made his position clear – he would support (the war) without hesitation.* ❜ (**A**)

The other parties put their support behind the war effort. Keir Hardie, a leading Labour politician, said:

❛ *A nation must be united ... with the boom of enemy guns within earshot the lads who have gone forth to fight must not be disheartened by any discordant note at home.* ❜ (**B**)

German attacks on Britain helped to unite the nation. In the winter of 1914-15, their fleet used the long, dark nights to cross the North Sea and shell the English coast. Hartlepool and Scarborough suffered and 500 people were killed or injured. **C** and **D** show the shock these events caused.

When war broke out, women were still not allowed to vote. There had been strong protests about this before the war, and now the women's leaders decided on action

C   A newspaper report on the shelling of Scarborough

D   After Scarborough, the recruitment campaign gained strength

by organizing a demonstration in London to show that they were willing and able to help with the war effort.

Lloyd George wrote in his war memoirs:

❛ *On 18th July 1915, they* (the 'suffragettes' who campaigned for votes for women) *headed a great women's war pageant in which thousands of women demonstrators marched for miles along London streets through mud and rain escorting a deputation that would meet me as Minister of Munitions to offer their services to help the country. Mrs Pankhurst (the Suffragette leader) also put in a plea for wage conditions that would safeguard their standard of living and prevent them being exploited by manufacturers. In reply I gave a guarantee that they should have a fair minimum wage and should receive for piece work the same rates as were paid for men ... These conditions had a permanent effect on the status of women workers in this country.* ❜ (**E**)

There were problems. Women earned less than men, and in spite of Lloyd George's guarantee of a fair minimum wage there was underpayment and exploitation.

❛ *Trade Unionists objected that women would lower men's wages ... yet women generally earned less than men. In the national shell factories the top wage for men was £4.6s.6d (£4.32½) that for women was £2.4s.6d.*

(£2.22½). By the end of 1915 the munitions plants were employing three women to one man but still at one Croydon factory the women who replaced men earning £3 weekly received 12s 6d (62½p). At Limehouse, women worked in a steaming basement shop dealing with food which was often vile-smelling and decomposing. **(F)**

So many extra people were employed, and so much extra material such as steel and explosives was needed, that the war effort was expensive. Taxes had to be increased to meet part of the cost, and people were encouraged to lend money to the government by buying war bonds. It was put to the people that it was their duty to lend as much as they could afford. Prices of basic foods rose sharply, and one of the complaints was that 'war pro-fiteers' were getting rich as a result. Between summer 1914 and summer 1915, the price rises were:

> *meat* – 40 per cent
> *bread* – 40 per cent
> *sugar* – 68 per cent
> *fish* – 60 per cent
> *flour* – 45 per cent

Generally, however, people were making an all-out effort to support Britain.

Recruitment

Thousands of men volunteered for service at the outbreak of war. They reported at recruiting offices set up in every town, took an oath in which they promised to fight 'for King and country' and accepted a shilling (5p) as a token of the agreement. As **G** suggests some were really not old enough:

The sergeant asked me my age and when told replied 'Clear off, son, come back tomorrow and we'll see if you're nineteen, eh?'. So I turned up the next day and gave my age as nineteen . . . holding up my right hand I swore to fight for king and country. The sergeant winked as he gave me the king's shilling. **(G)**

G. Coppard, *With a Machine Gun to Cambrai*

Still more men were needed. Recruiting posters, such as **H** and **J**, were used to attract new volunteers. It soon became accepted that it was every man's duty to enlist to fight. Men not in uniform were taunted and presented with white feathers, the mark of cowardice:

. . . I was witness to the presentation of a white feather. The victims were two young men who were disturbed from reading their evening newspapers by three young women. 'Why don't you fellows enlist? Your King and Country want you. We don't.' One of the girls . . . dishonoured one of the young men by sticking a white feather in his button hole . . . **(K)**

Daddy, what did *YOU* do in the Great War?

WOMEN OF BRITAIN SAY – "GO!"

H J Recruiting posters like these encouraged men to 'do their duty' and enlist

When the flood of volunteers slowed down, the government was forced to introduce conscription (1916), and every fit man between 18 and 45 had to do military service.

To some, the idea of fighting and killing was horrific and evil. Those who were not prepared to fight were classed as 'conscientious objectors', and had to appear before a tribunal which would listen to their appeal. Many appeals were turned down and the objectors sent to France. If they refused to obey orders to fire, they themselves were sometimes shot. Other 'conchies' served willingly in front-line ambulance and stretcher-bearing units, accepting the same risks as the troops.

??????????????????

1 a Why was the shelling of towns by the German navy such a shock to the British?
b Why did the government try to play down news of the attacks?

2 Why do you think the prices of fish and sugar increased so much more than other food prices in 1914-15?

3 Design a poster which you think would unite people behind a war effort today.

4 Study **H** and **J**. How do they differ in the way they appeal? Which is more effective?

5 'It is braver to be a conscientious objector than to fight.' Do you agree? Discuss.
or
Why do you think the government was forced to introduce conscription in 1916?

11 Jellicoe at Jutland

A   Admiral Jellicoe on board the *Iron Duke*

In 1916, Admiral Jellicoe (**A**) led the British Grand Fleet into the major sea battle of the war. Imagine his worries, it might fall to him to issue orders which could in the space of two or three hours decide who won the war. The destruction of the British battle fleet would be a fatal blow.

The Germans and Britons were frustrated at the lack of action from their fleets. The new German commander, Reinhold Scheer, had tried to lure the British fleet out to sea, and British towns had been shelled, but no decisive moves had been made.

On 31 May 1916, both fleets put out to sea, not knowing that the other side was there. Map **B** shows their course. Beatty (British) and Hipper (German) came into contact in the early afternoon when both went to investigate a steamer. Beatty and Hipper were thought more daring than their commanding officers. Hipper retreated, hoping to draw Beatty into the path of the full German fleet. There was a running battle and ships were sunk. Beatty guessed the closeness of the German fleet. He sailed north, followed by the Germans. Look at **C**. Beatty had succeeded in drawing the German fleet into the path of

the British fleet. This tactic was known as 'crossing the T'. The Germans were sailing into a line of British ships over six miles long. They clashed, and several ships were sunk, including the *Invincible,* which broke in two. Only six survived out of a crew of 1062 (**D**). Confusion and danger faced the men on both sides. A German gunnery officer wrote:

> ❛ *While firing was on, observation was out of the question, masses of smoke round the turrets. Only the two gunnery officers could see the enemy, our shots raised water spouts twice as high as their ships . . .* ❜ (**E**)

Had Jellicoe sought a decisive battle, he would have lost greater numbers. Partial victory for Britain sent nearly 9000 sailors to the bottom of the sea.

A sailor on HMS *Neptune* wrote:

> ❛ *It is a curious sensation being under fire from long range. The time of flight (of the shells) seems more like thirty minutes than the thirty or so seconds it actually is. A great gush of flame breaks out from the enemy's guns some miles away. Then follows a pause during which . . . two or three tons of metal and explosive are hurtling towards you. We saw our shells hit an enemy ship, the red glow of a hit is extremely pleasant to look upon.* ❜ (**F**)

B   Approach to the Battle of Jutland

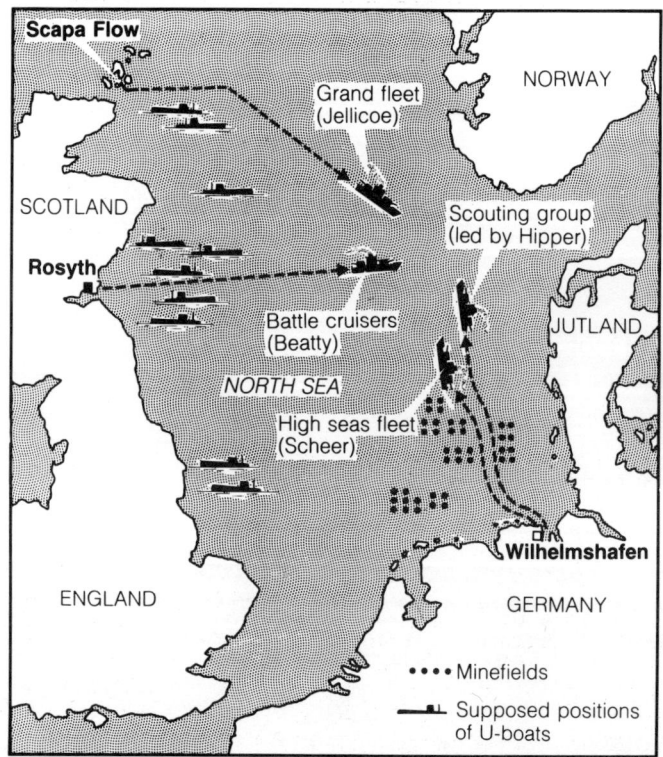

22

C Crossing the T: Jutland

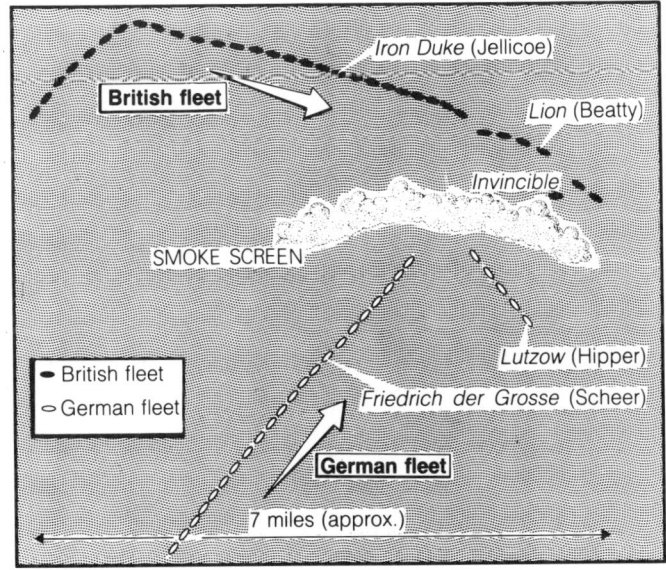

British fleet
- British fleet
- German fleet
Iron Duke (Jellicoe)
Lion (Beatty)
Invincible
SMOKE SCREEN
Lutzow (Hipper)
Friedrich der Grosse (Scheer)
German fleet
7 miles (approx.)

The German fleet was blocked in but later turned round again to shell the Grand Fleet. They then headed for port. A misty night aided their escape. Jellicoe did not know which course they would take. By the next morning, the Germans were back in port. Both Britain and Germany claimed victory. Kaiser Wilhelm II gave the German view:

‘ *The gigantic fleet of Albion, the ruler of the seas since Trafalgar came into the field. Our fleet engaged it. The British fleet was beaten. The cloud of British world supremacy has disappeared.* ’ **(G)**

The British were able to resume their blockade, but for some people this was not enough. Jellicoe was criticised for being too cautious and letting the Germans escape. He said afterwards:

D The sinking of *HMS Invincible*

‘ *If it had only been 6 o'clock instead of nearly dark, and clear, we should have had a second Trafalgar. I rejected at once the idea of night action ... owing firstly to the presence of torpedo craft and the impossibility of distinguishing between our own and enemy ships. Our search lights were not of the best type. Night fighting is pure chance.*

I missed one of the greatest opportunities a man ever had. ’ **(H)**

The Germans had better ships and guns. Smaller engines allowed heavier armour. The German steel was tougher, and their gun-sighting equipment was matchless in quality. The British took 121 hits with heavy shells, the Germans 55. The British had inadequate precautions to prevent fire spreading to the magazine below, which meant that a ship could be blown up by her own explosives.

J The battle line-up

	Britain	Germany
Battleships and heavy cruisers	37 (6 lost)	21 (2 lost)
Destroyers and light cruisers	113 (8 lost)	72 (9 lost)
Heavy guns	272	200
Men killed	6097	2551

???????????????????

1 Using the extracts explain why it was difficult for a commander to understand exactly what was happening during the battle of Jutland.

2 a Why was it important to 'cross the T'?
  b Look at the size of the fleets (**J**). Why was it difficult to command such fleets in battle?
  c Find two documents which a) refer to a previous British victory b) consider fighting at night to be risky. Find points over which the documents disagree.

3 Write a ship's log of the battle as it might have been seen by a sailor on either side. Start at the point where enemy ships are first sighted.

4 Analyse the figures in **J**. Why did the Germans claim that they had won?

5 Churchill described Jellicoe as 'the man who could have lost the war in an afternoon'. From Jellicoe's point of view, explain why you were cautious: mention weather, the time, German advantages, dangers to the British fleet, the chances of defeat.

12 The Eastern Front (1914-17)

A A Cossack scout: the ill-equipped Russian forces were no match for the highly-trained and technologically advanced German army

The Eastern Front differed from the Western in that armies moved great distances during their campaigns. A Russian army of seven and a half million men faced Austria and Germany in autumn 1914. The Allies called it 'the Russian steamroller' and thought that it would move unstoppably forward. If Germany's Schlieffen plan was to work, the steamroller would have to be halted.

Russian advance was held by men drawn from the Western Front, and German commanders Hindenburg and Ludendorff were helped in their defensive plans because they could easily decode Russian messages. In spite of their vast numbers of soldiers the Russian armies failed. Their military tactics and equipment were unable to match up to modern warfare (**A**). In some Russian units sent to the front, only about a quarter of the men had rifles. The rest had to pick up the rifles of the dead. A British soldier wrote of their hopeless position:

❛ *All the conditions of the moment were against them with the sole exception of numbers. They were already*

fighting against Austria ... they were undertaking the difficult task of manoeuvring separated forces against a concentrated enemy – modern weapons, motor transport, aeroplanes, wireless telephones would have eased the task, but Russia lacked these. ❜ (**B**)

Lloyd George, in his memoirs of the First World War, wrote:

❛ *If the Russians ever had a plan against Germany it never came off. The invasion of East Prussia was little more than a chivalrous improvisation to save France from the blunders of her generals.* ❜ (**C**)

When mutilated soldiers returned home with news of defeat because of lack of preparation, the mood was one of resentment against the government and the Allies. A typical village sent twenty-six young men to fight; only two returned. Russia asked why Britain, with her great industries, was unable to help with munitions.

In 1915, the Central Powers (Germany, Austria and their allies) attacked deep into Russia through the sort of countryside shown in **D**. There were great distances to be covered and the armies were spread more thinly than in Europe's front line. Food was short and the weather was bad. Many Russians surrendered rather than fight in the terrible conditions, and some men shot off their own trigger fingers to escape the horrors of hunger and sub-zero temperatures. Large numbers of prisoners were taken (**E**). An extract from a letter written by a Russian general from the front tells of the hardships and hopelessness:

D The German army advanced deep into Russia, in spite of the hostile environment

E A train full of Russian prisoners, after the battle of Tannenberg

❝ Would it be possible to increase the quantity of shells even if there's no fuses to explode them? They would keep the spirits of the men up. Many of the men are without boots and have frostbitten feet. They are without sweaters. When officers are killed mass surrenders start. They say 'Why should we perish of hunger and cold without boots, the artillery is silent, we are killed like partridges'. The cossacks recovered 500 men who had been captured. They were told 'Who asked you, fools. We do not want to hunger and freeze again.' ❞ **(F)**

Russia's fortunes changed briefly in June 1916 when General Brusilov successfully counter-attacked the Austrians and captured many prisoners. He was let down in the end by poor railway links, which meant that he could not get reinforcements fast enough. Germany was able to plug the gap made in the defences, and Austria was able to recover.

The ruler of Russia, Tsar Nicholas II, went to the front as commander-in-chief in 1916 in a desperate attempt to save the situation, but there was nothing he could do. Russia was having trouble of her own, and was near to revolution after many years of poverty and hunger under harsh, cruel governments.

The small Russian air force ran a double risk. It had to face a superior enemy, and was shot at by its own soldiers who saw so few aircraft that they could not tell friend from foe.

Overall, Russia's army strength in 1914 was 7 480 000 men. Only 4 625 000 rifles were available, when 11 000 000 were needed for immediate use and to replace those damaged and lost in the fighting. An order for 3 500 000 was placed with suppliers in the USA in 1915, but two years later only one tenth of this number had been received. Heavy machine guns ordered from the Vickers factory in England were not delivered until 1916.

By early 1917 German troops were deep in Russia (see map F on p. 30).

???????????????????

1 Why was 'steamroller' a good description for the Russian armies?

2 As a Russian general, write an explanation of why you have done so badly in the campaigns of 1914-15.

3 From looking at the figures above could the west have done more to help Russia?

4 Imagine you are a Russian soldier who has just surrendered to an Austrian patrol. Explain why you have given up without a fight.

5 What evidence is there that Russia tried to help an ally?

13 Blunder and failure: Gallipoli

B Gallipoli: Gateway to Turkey

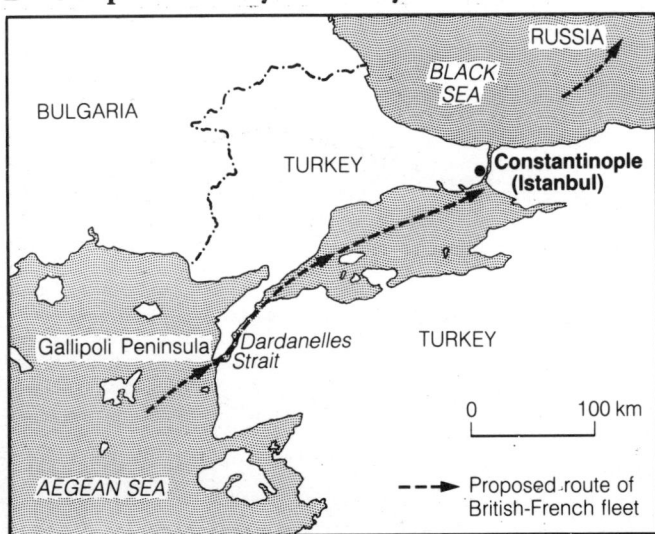

There was deadlock on the Western Front in 1915, and a search began to find other battle fronts. Churchill and Kitchener favoured an attack on Turkey. She seemed an easy target and any victory would be good for morale. From **A** you can work out other reasons why the British war cabinet decided to support this plan. A member wrote:

❝ *If we can take Gallipoli, Rumania, Greece and probably Bulgaria will declare for us. (These) would throw an army of 1 500 000 on to the Austrian flank. This would not only relieve pressure on Russia but indirectly on France. This will give time to re-equip the Russian army.* ❞ **(A)**

Churchill was certain that a naval force was all that was needed. Map **B** shows the route the fleet was to take to Constantinople (Istanbul), the Turkish capital. On 18 March 1915, British and French ships moved into the Dardanelles. They dealt with the shore defences, but at the end of the first day three ships had been sunk. It was not known until much later that they had been sunk by mines. Admiral de Roebuck decided to retreat.

On 18 April 1915, armies led by Sir Iain Hamilton attempted to land on the Gallipoli peninsula by attacking various bays (**C**). Australian and New Zealand troops were used. The Turks were expecting an attack, and thousands of the Allied troops were killed before reaching the shore. The sea turned red with blood. Hamilton commanded his men from a ship, which meant he could not co-ordinate the action in every bay. A soldier tells of the resulting confusion:

❝ *To sum up our failure to capture Constantinople in one week ... Y and S beach forces outnumbered the whole Turkish forces opposing the five landings. On 25th April S force remained inactive all day, the force at V beach was annihilated.*

One mile round the coast at W beach a landing was made at great cost. At Y beach, an hour's march away, 2000 men landed and sat around all day waiting.

What a waste, just because of the absence of information about what was happening on other beaches.

No, you cannot win a battle by remote control from the sea. The Turks did not beat us, we beat ourselves. Our commanders were out of touch, out of date, out of sympathy ... ❞ **(D)**

The troops dug in, in positions such as those shown in **E**. The positions were difficult to defend because they were overlooked by higher ground. Trench conditions were bad. The army had allowed for heat by shipping water all the way from Egypt, but there was a plague of flies which made life miserable, as a soldier remembers:

❝ *The flies – for breakfast there is salty bacon and fly tea. As one opens a tin the flies are so thick they are squashed in the process. One never sees the jam, one can only see a blue-black mixture of sticky, sickly flies. They drink our sweat and our lips and eyes are covered with them.* ❞ **(F)**

The heat of summer slowly gave way before the bitter cold of winter. This was something the planners had not

C 'V' beach, Gallipoli

26

E Australian and New Zealand troops 'dug-in' at Gallipoli

anticipated. An officer wrote to a member of the government:

❝ I am still hoping to hear that the corrugated iron (for shelters) has at last arrived. It had not reached us at the time of the Great Blizzard when hundreds of men died from exposure, frost and drowning. ❞ **(G)**

The same officer complained of Hamilton's inefficiency, and the unnecessary sacrifice of lives:

❝ Why, when a landing was possible at the dunes of Suvla, did he land at Helles? He threw us into the mountains at the toe of the peninsula … the point furthest from Constantinople. Had the original landing taken place at Suvla it would have cost a tenth of the men lost at Helles. ❞ **(H)** (Suvla and Helles are bays.)

Hamilton missed several opportunities. On one occasion, after taking a small force of Turks by surprise, the advancing troops were allowed to settle down for breakfast. By the time the meal was over, large numbers of Turkish riflemen had gathered. At Suvla Bay, 20 000 men landed. Their commanding officer, Stopford, did not go ashore. After congratulating his men on the success of the landing, it is claimed that he 'went off for his afternoon nap'.

All Allied troops had been pulled out of Gallipoli by the end of January 1915. Over half the total force of half a million had become casualties, and nothing had been gained. There was much discussion about who was to blame. Churchill resigned from his position of responsibility for the navy, but Hamilton refused to accept any blame.

Commander Keyes later said that a successful campaign at Gallipoli might have shortened the war by two years and saved millions of lives. As it is, Gallipoli and places like Suvla Bay and Anzac Cove are remembered for blunders and failure.

???????????????????

1 It is said that defeating Turkey would have given the allies a back door into Germany. What do you think this means?

2 You are a member of the war cabinet in January 1915. Write a short speech to persuade your colleagues to support the attack on Turkey.

3 Using all the evidence on this page, list the mistakes which the British command made. What excuses could they make?

4 In your opinion, was the Gallipoli campaign a good idea in the first place? Give reasons for your answer.

14 A Worldwide War

A Soldiers of the '9th Hodson's Horse', 1917

The Great War, as it was called at the time, is now usually referred to as the First World War. Most of the action was in Europe, but the effects were worldwide. Troops were drawn from all corners of the British Empire (**A**), and nations friendly to Britain looked after its interests in their own territory. The large German military presence in South-west Africa surrendered unconditionally to General Botha, which meant an end to the threat of danger from that part of the world (**B**).

Germany lost the area of China which it controlled, and Japan (which had joined the Allied cause) seized German island possessions in the Pacific Ocean. There was a furious response in the official German war news:

❛ *Woe to you, Japan. England has betrayed the white races in the surrender of Tsing Tau to the Japanese. There is no honour for England or Japan in having taken Tsing Tau, which was defended by only 6000 Germans, with tenfold superiority. The day of reckoning with Japan will be long postponed but our time will come.* ❜ (**C**)

Italy, which remained neutral in 1914, signed a secret treaty in London in 1915. It promised to help Britain and France in return for large areas of the Austrian empire. Britain was keen on Italy's co-operation for a reason which army commander Lord Kitchener made obvious in a letter to one of his generals:

B News of the surrender of the German forces in South-west Africa

SOUTH-WEST AFRICA SURRENDERS.

ENTIRE GERMAN ARMY IN GENERAL BOTHA'S HANDS.

HIS TRIUMPHAL CAMPAIGN.

COUNTRY HALF AS LARGE AGAIN AS GERMANY.

UNION CITIZEN FORCE RETURNING.

Mr. Bonar Law, Colonial Secretary, received yesterday the following telegram from Lord Buxton, Governor-General of the Union of South Africa :—

Following has been officially communicated to Press from Defence Headquarters, Pretoria :—This morning, July 9, at 2 o'clock, General Botha accepted Governor Seitz's surrender of all the German forces

28

‘ *I suppose we must now recognise that the French Army cannot make a sufficient break in the German lines. Russia is hard pressed. Fresh troops are needed to break the deadlock. Italy and Rumania seem the most likely providers.* ’ (**D**)

Fighting was not easy (**E**). King Victor Emmanuel of Italy wrote:

‘ *Picture to yourself my men 3000 metres up in the clouds for seven months in deep snow ... imagine the difficulties of such life* ’ (**F**)

The Italians made little progress. Morale began to sink. In October 1917, disaster struck. The Austrians began an advance at Caporetto, and with them were some crack German troops transferred from the Western Front. The Italians were confused. They panicked and retreated seventy miles in seven days. The advance was stopped at the River Piave. **G** was written by a British soldier. It explains one factor which helped the Italians.

‘ *November 1917, the Western Front ... we were moving to another front ... after a long train journey ... we knew Italy was our destination ... In conjunction with other brigades and with French troops we could be deployed to meet further enemy penetration.* ’ (**G**)

The shame of Caporetto was not easily forgotten by the Allies, but Senator Camastra justified Italy's position in a letter to the *Daily Telegraph*:

‘ *The criticism of British statement does not extinguish the glory of (the Italian) army. Similar episodes (to Caporetto) occurred during the war on various allied fronts, but these were given little publicity compared to Caporetto.*

The facts are different to the legend ... When the allies arrived in Italy the Italian army had unaided halted the advancing forces.

The Italian army, after driving back the invading forces, regained yard by yard the lost territory, crowning with the heroic decisive battle at Vittorio Veneto. ’ (**H**)

In 1918 the Italians had considerable success, taking over 300 000 Austrians prisoner at the battle of Vittorio Veneto. Altogether, over 500 000 Italians died during the war.

In the Middle East, Britain was helped by the Arabs, who were glad to fight against their Turkish rulers. Lawrence of Arabia (T.E. Lawrence) was one of the British soldiers who persuaded the Arabs to revolt. As **J** shows, this war was very different from that in the trenches:

‘ *Our tent was made with tarpaulin drawn over petrol cans. A bunch of dirty Arabs came down the pass on camels. Their leader in his white headdress spoke: 'My*

E   Italian soldiers in the snow, near Caporetto

name is Lawrence, I have come to join you' ... On our journeys he told me of the difficulties ... We had three methods of progress – to bluff, buy or fight our way through. ’ (**J**)

In 1917 and 1918, the fall of such famous towns as Baghdad, Jerusalem and Damascus thrilled people in Britain. Lawrence describes entering Damascus:

‘ *When we came in there had been some miles of people. Now every man, woman and child was in the streets. Damascus went mad with joy – women tore off their veils – householders threw flowers and carpets in the street.* ’ (**K**)

America entered the war in 1917, making it worldwide.

??????????????????

1 What is the significance of the soldiers' clothing in the photograph of the mountain outpost? Would it have been suitable on the Western Front?

2 **H** mentions 'similar episodes (to Caporetto)'. Name some.

3 Do you think **H** is a reliable source? Give reasons.

4 Locate on a world map all the places mentioned in this section. In your opinion, could the Great War be described as a 'world' war?

5 The Arabs were part of the Ottoman or Turkish Empire, from which they wanted to break free. What event would help them to believe that Britain was a safe ally?

6 Why was it not possible for Germany to go to the aid of her colonies in the Pacific, China and South-west Africa?

15 The Year of Change: 1917

There was still deadlock on several fronts in 1917. By the end of the year, Russia had become a communist country, shortly to leave the war, and America had joined the Allies.

For the reasons given in section 12 (*The Eastern Front*), Russia was doing badly in the war. By 1917, the troops at the front were losing heart. An English nurse serving with the Russians wrote:

❮ *23rd Jan 1917 Sabotage – railroads destroyed, workshops looted. Mobs shouting 'Peace and bread'. They are aware the war is at the root of their hardships. The Tsar wishes to please everybody and pleases no-one. We are amazed at newspapers criticising the governments. A few months ago the writers would have been arrested. Things cannot continue as they are.* ❯ (**A**)

On 2 March 1917 the Tsar abdicated, leaving the country to be run by a temporary government. The Tsar said:

❮ *The internal disturbances threaten the war effort. The destiny of Russia, the honour of our heroic army, the welfare of the people demand that we win the war. The hour is already close when our army will be able to overwhelm the enemy completely. In these decisive days, to draw our people together, we have decided to abdicate the throne.* ❯ (**B**)

The Provisional Government of Prince Lvov and Alexander Kerensky tried to carry on the war. They faced many problems. The food shortages remained. The Communists were spreading revolutionary ideas among the workers and troops. Lenin, leader of the Bolsheviks (a Communist group), was helped by the Germans to return from Switzerland to Russia. His slogan was 'land, peace and bread', which appealed to the oppressed peasants and war-weary soldiers. The Bolsheviks believed:

❮ *It is not possible to end the war by the ending of activities by the soldiers of one side. We therefore encourage the fraternization of soldiers. This can lead to revolution in all of the countries which are now fighting.* ❯ (**C**)

An army intelligence report stated:

❮ *Everywhere one hears voices calling for peace because no one will stay in the trenches in the winter. The Germans use leaflets and newspapers to encourage fraternization.* ❯ (**D**)

E   Russian and Austrian soldiers sharing soup

Russian and Austrian soldiers put aside their weapons and met as friends (**E**).

In October 1917, Lenin and the Bolsheviks seized power. They soon began peace negotiations, and the Treaty of Brest-Litovsk was signed in March 1918. Map **F** shows the extent of Russia's loss of land under the treaty – one third of its wheat-growing areas, one third of its railways, a quarter of its population and three quarters of its heavy industry. German troops were allowed to occupy the area, and to harvest the wheat in 1918.

Britain and France sent troops to help the non-communist or 'White' Russians fight the Bolsheviks, and Germany concentrated its forces once again on the Western Front.

F   Results of the Treaty of Brest-Litovsk

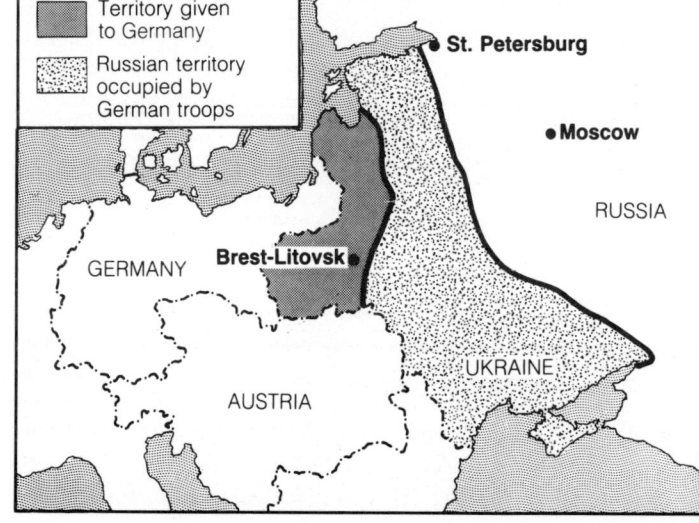

The entry into the war of the USA balanced the loss of Russia. The USA had never been involved before as an ally in European wars, and had remained neutral in 1914. Many Americans were of German descent and approved of the policy of 'isolation'. However American business interests realised that big profits could be made by trading with Europe, and goods were soon pouring across the Atlantic. The sinking of the passenger ship *Lusitania* had caused some anti-German feeling, but President Wilson tried to counter this when he presented himself for re-election in 1916. Part of his campaign was based on the idea of keeping out of the fight (**G**). The people of America seemed to support the idea of peace and Wilson was returned as President.

The year after his election, Wilson declared war on Germany. Cartoon **H** is a comment on his U-turn. In his war speech to congress, Wilson gave his reasons:

❝ *Vessels of every kind, whatever their flag, their cargo, their destination, their errand, have been ruthlessly sent to the bottom without warning or thought of help – the vessels of friendly neutrals, even hospital ships.*

Since the start of the war the Germans have had spies here in America. Now she means to stir up enemies at our very doors.

The world must be made safe for democracy. ❞ (**J**)

Although Wilson made it seem a matter of conscience, there were business reasons. If Germany sank the ships, trade would stop. This would mean unemployment in America. Depression could set in. If the Allies lost the war, they would not pay back the money America had lent them.

There was another reason too. Source **K** is part of a telegram sent by the German Foreign Secretary, Zimmerman, to his Ambassador in Mexico. It was decoded by the British who leaked it to the Americans.

G A truck used in President Wilson's election campaign: 'Who keeps us out of war?'

H An American cartoon commenting on Wilson's about-turn

❝ *We intend to begin unrestricted submarine warfare. If there is a war with the USA, we will offer Mexico an alliance – Make war on our side, and Mexico can re-conquer the lost territory of Texas, New Mexico and Arizona.* ❞ (**K**)

What help did the Americans give? They needed time to recruit, train and send over their armies. They had few munitions factories, tanks or aeroplanes, but their navy was quickly in use in the Atlantic. American money loans were most useful. Most of all, they gave the Allies a boost in morale and a hope of victory in 1918.

??????????????????

1 Do you think that the Tsar is telling the whole truth in **B**?

2 Would you say that the main aim of the Bolsheviks was to make peace with Germany and Austria or to throw out the Russian government? Give reasons.

3 In what ways did the USA hope to protect herself by entering a war which was being fought over three thousand miles away? How might that war have touched mainland America?

4 What does **D** show about the attitude of Russian soldiers on the Eastern Front?

5 What do you think cartoon **H** is trying to say about America and President Wilson's attitude to the war?

6 American 'draft-dodgers' were imprisoned for refusing to fight. Write a letter, as from a parent, persuading a son of the reasons in favour of fighting.

16 War at Home (2)

A   Members of the Women's Land Army

Men in the trenches talked about returning to 'Blighty', which was home in Britain. A soldier arriving here on leave late in the war would notice changes as soon as he got off the train – there were women porters and guards. Women were working as tram conductors, coal merchants and members of fire brigades. They were doing factory and agricultural work (**A**) – all areas of traditional male employment. Sisters and wives might shock returning soldiers by smoking in public, drinking in bars or wearing trousers when not at work.

The Defence of the Realm Act (known as DORA), passed by the government, gave it power over the railways and mines and enabled it to make changes to help the war effort. This was often inconvenient for the public.

DORA was used to stop the throwing of bread to pigeons – there was to be no waste. The government had tried to stop strikes. Lloyd George, Minister of Munitions, was keen on this ban because it was his job to keep the soldiers supplied with shells. There were strikes for more pay in Clydeside and South Wales. Newspapers expressed disgust for the strikers (**B**).

There was another side to the strikes, as a union official explained:

❛ . . . we, the Clyde engineers, thought our demand was so reasonable that if we struck, public opinion would be with us. We thought they would think it wrong that American engineers were being paid 26 shillings more than British engineers. But we were wrong. People said I was a traitor and should be shot. However, when Lloyd George visited our works I warned him that to us the Munitions Act was making us slaves. ❜ (**C**)

The government had acted after it had seemed that the war effort was being held up by too much drinking. Drinking hours were introduced, and it was forbidden to 'treat' your friends in public houses. The king set a good example by taking a pledge to give up drink.

A soldier returning home to one of the big cities, London in particular, would hope that his home had not been destroyed by a German *Zeppelin,* a large airship which could carry bombs. About 1600 people were killed in bombing raids, and much damage was caused. Anti-German riots (**D**) followed the raids, and feelings ran high. The king, who was related to the German royal family, changed his name from Hanover to Windsor, and others with German-sounding names followed his example.

The U-boat campaign had made food supplies short. Viscountess Rhondda remembers:

❛ My father was made Food Controller in June 1917. The job killed him in a year. During January and February 1918 as many as a million people were standing in queues for food which often went before the last could get their share. January 25th: Butter and magarine queues, meat queues and a new development, fish queues. On February 25th 1918, the rationing plan started. The queues disappeared. They never returned. ❜ (**E**)

B   Many newspapers condemned the strikers

SCANDAL OF THE CLYDE STRIKE

NAVY SUPPLIES HELD UP
FOR A CONCERT
IN A CINEMA HALL

DEAF TO PATRIOTISM.

MINIMUM OF WORK
TO BE DONE
BY SOME OF THE MEN.

D Anti-German riots in the East End of London

Poster campaigns encouraged people to economise (**F**). Sugar, meat and butter were rationed. Beer production was cut, and the grain that was saved was made into flour for bread. 'Allotments' were made available – small plots of land for food-growing. The king and Lloyd George set an example by growing food on their own land. The newly-introduced 'summertime' daylight-saving plan meant that it was possible to work late for several months of the year.

Soldiers resented the men who stayed at home without good reason and 'got rich quick', making use of their knowledge of business to turn wartime conditions to their advantage. Then there was the difficulty of talking to people who had not seen the horrors of war and simply did not understand conditions at the front: Robert Graves wrote:

❛ *England looked strange to us returned soldiers. We could not understand the war madness The people talked the 'newspaper language'. I could not talk to my parents. At my wedding reception there was a three-tiered wedding cake. The Nicholsons had saved for a month to make it taste like a real one. But when the plaster icing was lifted the guests sighed with disappointment. After three drinks, Nancy (his new wife) went off to change into her land girl's smock.* ❜ (**G**)

The war effort demanded sacrifices and imposed hardship, but the general response from the public was good. Deep down, there was a longing for peace, which finally came on 11 November 1918, a date we remember as Poppy Day. Winston Churchill tells how London reacted to the announcement that the war was over:

❛ *. . . I looked into the street. It was deserted. Then from all sides men and women came into the street. The bells began to clash. Thousands rushing in a frantic manner, shouting, screaming. Flags appeared . . . London streets were in pandemonium.* ❜ (**H**)

We risk our lives to bring you food. It's up to you not to waste it.

'A Message from our Seamen'

F Posters like this encouraged people to economise on food

??????????????????????

1 Why do you think the sign on the shop in **D** reads 'We are Russians'?

2 As a woman in 1918, write to your MP explaining why you should be allowed to vote.

3 Design a poster to encourage people to save meat or sugar.

4 Why was it necessary to economise on food?

5 What was the writer of **C** trying to say? Do you think he should have been concerned about anything other than producing war materials, whatever the cost to him?

6 In 1914, people cheered as war started. Explain why in 1918, they cheered as it ended.

c

17 War in the Air

To people at the time, the war in the air was exciting and interesting in spite of the danger. Londoners used to gaze up at Zeppelins about to bomb them. Few had seen an aircraft in 1914; it was only five years since Louis Blériot had become the first man to fly the English Channel.

Little thought had been given to the use of aircraft in battle. The German generals' view was:

❢ *Experience has shown that a real combat in the air such as journalists and romancers have described should be considered a myth. The duty of the aviator is to see, not to fight.* ❢ **(A)**

In other words, the purpose of the aircraft was to fly over the enemy lines and report troop positions and movements.

The Germans used the Zeppelin airship to observe the Allies, especially in the North Sea. From 1915 onwards, Zeppelins bombed British cities. This was a new departure in warfare. Like the shelling of towns in the north-east of England by the Germany navy, it caused shock and alarm to the population. People had accepted the idea that the Royal Navy would be able to keep civilians safe. In this account of a Zeppelin raid on London, the writer admits her interest in the scene:

❢ *From the balcony we saw the long, sinuous airship, lit up by the searchlights. While we were being pleasantly excited by it, women and children were being killed and maimed.* ❢ **(B)**

Closer to the impact, the scene was one of destruction. This is how a theatre call boy remembers it:

❢ *As the first bomb exploded people were flung in all directions. One woman was blown to pieces, another cut in two by a piece of glass. One man clutching a sandwich was found half outside, half inside a saloon bar.* ❢ **(C)**

From the government announcement, **D,** you can work out the precautions which the government took against the raids.

❢ *Last night's raid was carried out by thirteen ships. The new measure for obscuring lights was effective and the airships groped about in the darkness. Three airships approached London. One was picked up by searchlights and engaged by anti-aircraft guns and aeroplanes. It burst into flames. Our experts are trying to reconstruct the wreckage. The amount of wood is startling and would point to a shortage of aluminium in Germany.* ❢ **(D)**

E A British naval airship escorting a convoy

Britain developed its own airships. **E** shows one escorting a convoy. Both sides used airships on the Western Front for observation work and for directing artillery fire. By 1918, airships were massive, the largest Zeppelins being over 200 metres long and powered by as many as six engines.

The real romance was reserved for aeroplanes. Each side used them in the early days of war for observation. The machines were flimsy. Their defences were a revolver, rifle or hand-held machine gun. Some carried bombs which had to be picked up and dropped over the side by hand. At first, pilots on both sides took a 'gentlemanly' attitude to each other. A British airman wrote:

❢ *The first time I met a German machine both the pilot and myself were unarmed. We were photographing the trenches when I saw a German two-seater below. The German observer did not appear to be shooting at us. We waved a hand. The enemy did likewise. This did not seem ridiculous – there is a bond of sympathy between all who fly – even enemies.* ❢ **(G)**

F A Morane Parasol monoplane, which was used on bombing raids against the Germans

The mood changed in late 1915 and 1916. The new planes had space only for a pilot. What reasons can you think of for why the pilots preferred to fly without observers? **H** shows a German Fokker triplane. You can just see the fitted machine gun. It now had to be fired by the pilot.

Dogfights were fought across the skies of northern France. Speed and manoeuvrability were most important. This is from the memoirs of a German airman:

❛ Suddenly two machines jump up before me. I cannot rely on my engine now – A couple of shots – gun jammed – yes, it would – I feel defenceless and in my rage I try to ram an enemy's machine. I bear down on him. I press the trigger buttons – the guns begin to fire again. I see the observer and pilot lurch forward. Their plane crashes in a shellhole – the other Englishman vanishes – I try to steer home with a compass before my petrol runs out. ❜ (**J**)

The same man examines a captured British plane: 'A beautiful plane – so much brass and rubber – poor Germany – no brass at all on our machines and our flying schools have wooden wheels'.

Each side tried to build the best planes, striving for the extra bit of speed, power and ability to turn and climb which would give an advantage over the enemy. The skill of the pilots hit the newspapers, and each side honoured its aces: Ball and Mannock for Britain, Guynemer and Fonck for France, Immelmann and Voss for Germany. The most famous was the German Baron von Richthofen. His groups of pilots (known as a 'circus') painted their machines bright red. Others carried the pilot's name in large letters. Pilots often annoyed their officers because they did not wear proper uniform, as photograph **K** shows.

Behind the glory, there was danger. Von Richthofen said:

H   A German Fokker triplane

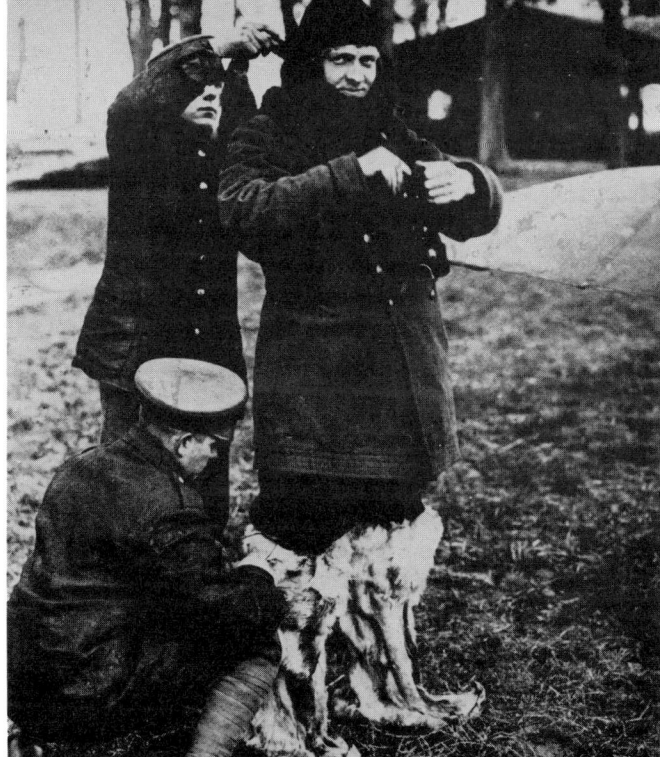

K   Baron von Richthofen preparing for a flight

❛ I am a hunter; when I have shot down an Englishman my passion is satisfied for a quarter of an hour ❜ (**L**)

Machines often failed, there were no parachutes and casualties were high. In April 1917, the average life of a front-line pilot was two weeks. Between March and May of that year, 1270 planes of the Royal Flying Corps were shot down, but volunteers still came forward.

On 1 April 1918, the Royal Flying Corps (army) and the Royal Naval Air Service (navy) were combined to form the Royal Air Force.

??????????????????

1 Which evidence suggests that the British blockade of enemy ports was hitting the German war effort?

2 Look at photograph **H**. What problem was faced by the engineers who decided to mount the machine gun in that particular position?

3 What evidence is there that pilots considered themselves to be an elite – a rather special group of men? Why should they take this attitude?

4 Work out from **D** what precautions the British government took against air raids.

5 If you were a soldier asking for a transfer to the Royal Flying Corps, how would you answer the question 'Why do you want to join?'

6 Which would you consider to be more effective in the war: airship or aircraft? Give reasons.

18 The Spring Offensives, 1918

Towards the end of March 1918, the Germans decided to launch their gamble for victory in the form of a knockout blow on the Western Front. German commander General Ludendorff tells why:

❛ *The situation in Russia and Italy makes it possible to deliver a blow on the Western Front in the New Year. Our general situation requires that we should strike at the earliest possible moment before the Americans can throw strong forces in.* ❜ (**A**)

There were other reasons, hinted at in these words by a German civilian:

❛ *One of the most terrible sufferings was having to sit in the dark. It became dark at four ... it was not light till eight in the morning. Even the children could not sleep that long. When they went to bed we were left shivering with the chill that comes from semi-starvation.* ❜ (**B**)

At first, the attack was successful. The British and French troops were hit by a heavy barrage from the German artillery. The Germans used specially-trained 'storm-troopers'. Armed with portable trench mortars, flame throwers, stick bombs and light machine guns they tore through the Allied lines in the early morning mist. In ten days, they moved forty miles into the Allied territory. There were trying to split the Allies. By 1 June they were only thirty-seven miles from Paris. An account by a British officer shows the British concern:

❛ *The roads were fairly full and this time while it would be wrong to say there was a panic the retreat resembled a rout. Everyone seemed anxious to get away as quickly as possible regardless of anyone else. A few military policemen dashed up and down but no-one took much notice. Had the Germans been able to break through with cavalry or armoured cars the war would have ended for us.* ❜ (**C**)

Another Battle of the Marne was fought and the German attack was halted. French Marshal Foch (**D**) had been made supreme commander, which meant that he could control and co-ordinate all the Allied troops on the Western Front. Their combined efforts brought success.

General Haig made a 'fight to the last man' appeal to the British troops:

The Germans had problems which took much of the power from their attacks. A German soldier remembers:

D   Marshal Foch (*right*) and Sir Douglas Haig, inspecting soldiers of the Gordon Highlanders

E   Haig's 'order of the day' appeal to his forces

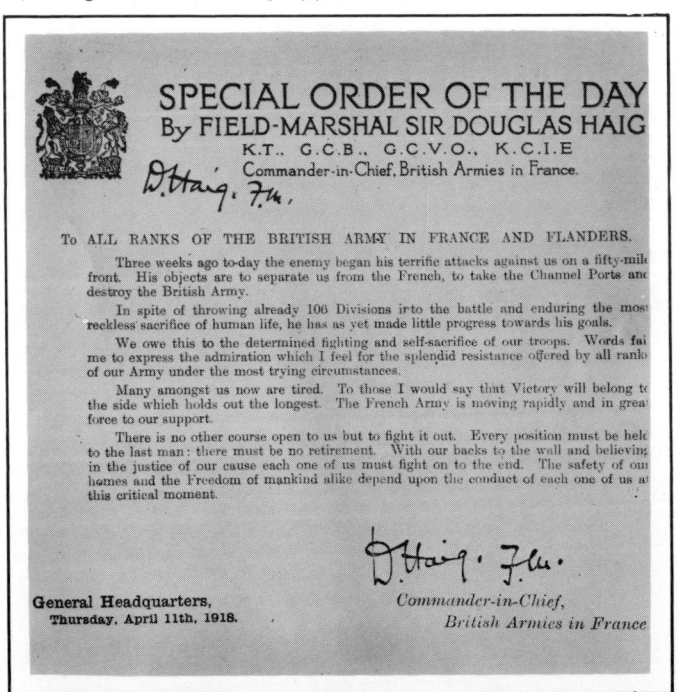

SPECIAL ORDER OF THE DAY
By FIELD-MARSHAL SIR DOUGLAS HAIG
K.T., G.C.B., G.C.V.O., K.C.I.E
Commander-in-Chief, British Armies in France.

D. Haig. F.M.

To ALL RANKS OF THE BRITISH ARMY IN FRANCE AND FLANDERS.

Three weeks ago to-day the enemy began his terrific attacks against us on a fifty-mile front. His objects are to separate us from the French, to take the Channel Ports and destroy the British Army.

In spite of throwing already 106 Divisions into the battle and enduring the most reckless sacrifice of human life, he has as yet made little progress towards his goals.

We owe this to the determined fighting and self-sacrifice of our troops. Words fail me to express the admiration which I feel for the splendid resistance offered by all ranks of our Army under the most trying circumstances.

Many amongst us now are tired. To those I would say that Victory will belong to the side which holds out the longest. The French Army is moving rapidly and in great force to our support.

There is no other course open to us but to fight it out. Every position must be held to the last man: there must be no retirement. With our backs to the wall and believing in the justice of our cause each one of us must fight on to the end. The safety of our homes and the Freedom of mankind alike depend upon the conduct of each one of us at this critical moment.

D. Haig. F.M.

General Headquarters,
Thursday, April 11th, 1918.

*Commander-in-Chief,
British Armies in France*

H American troops arriving at Le Havre, July 1918

❛ *The physical exhaustion of the men was so great that they could not fire their rifles. They let themselves be wiped out almost without caring or moving . . . We are glad if the ration carts can get up to us at night – then the men and horses feed for the next twenty-four hours at one sitting. All the water we can get comes from the icy shell holes. (There was looting). I see men carrying hens under their arms, men wearing top hats, men carrying wine bottles, men who could hardly walk.* ❜ (**F**)

German armour was in short supply:

❛ *We had no tanks . . . our attacks succeeded without them, says Ludendorff. It is not precisely true that the Germans had no tanks at all . . . but they never employed more than thirteen on a single occasion. Not only did they not produce tanks for their great offensive. Armoured cars were equally absent and to the best of my knowledge so were motorised machine guns (carried in motorcycle sidecars) which the British certainly possessed.* ❜ (**G**)

In the summer of 1918, the Allies received a great boost to morale when American troops arrived (**H**). This is how a French officer remembers the occasion:

❛ *They passed in columns closely packed in motor lorries, bareheaded, bare chested, singing American songs at the tops of their voices amid the cheers of onlookers. These magnificent youths from across the sea, radiating health, produced a great effect.* ❜ (**J**)

In the forty days since the German attack, over 700 000

men had been killed or wounded. General Haig discussed the next stage of the war with Churchill:

❛ *I told him (Churchill) we ought to do our utmost to get a decision this autumn. We are engaged in a 'wearing-out' battle. If we allow the enemy a period of quiet he will recover and the wearing-out process must be recommenced. In reply I was told that General Staff in London calculate that the decisive stage of the war will not arise until next July.* ❜ (**K**)

???????????????????

1 What evidence is there that both sides were finding it hard to keep discipline?

2 Why does Ludendorff feel able to say in **A** that the situation in Russia and Italy makes it possible to deliver a blow to the Western Front?

3 Why was it an advantage for the Allied forces to have a supreme commander? Why do you think that nobody had been appointed earlier?

4 What problems for German civilians are hinted at in **B**?

5 General Haig spoke to Churchill in August 1918 (**K**), saying that he wanted to fight on without a break. Why do you think that the planners preferred to wait for almost a year?

19 The Allied Victory, 1918

A The Final Offensive, Autumn 1918

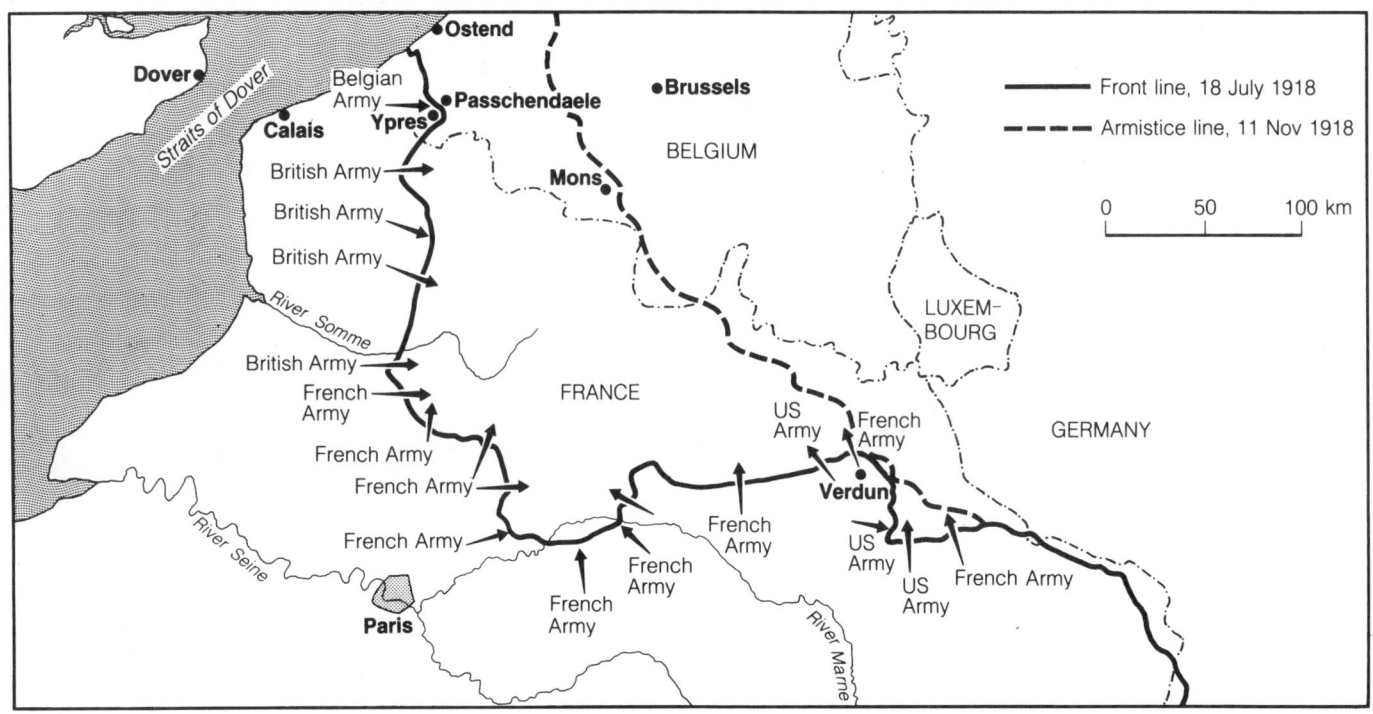

The Allied armies of the British, French and Americans began their counter-attacks in August 1918, along a line which stretched from the Belgian coast almost to Switzerland (**A**). This quotation from the *Frankfurter Zeitung* newspaper shows the German attitude to the situation:

❛ During these weeks of the counter-offensive we remain without anxiety for the German front which is strong and strategically indestructible. If at certain places the enemy has been able to push forward this is solely due to our plans which are for more attacks, which are of course only interrupted for the time being. ❜ (**B**)

The Allies had the use of tanks (**C**) which had serious drawbacks from the point of view of their crews:

❛ Of the thirty-eight tanks that went into action on the eleventh all need overhauling; the crews are completely exhausted ... the pulses of one crew were taken immediately they got out of their tank. The beats averaged 130 to the minute or twice as fast as they should have been. Two men temporarily lost their reason and had to be held back by force. One tank commander became delirious. In some cases where infantry were carried in the tank they fainted within three quarters of an hour from the start. It is clear that the tank was not a war-winning weapon. ❜ (**D**)

The Germans saw them in a different light:

❛ The enemy made use of tanks in large numbers. They suddenly emerged from smoke clouds. Our men were unnerved. Tanks broke through our front lines causing a panic which upset our battle control. When we were able to locate them our anti-tank guns and our artillery speedily put an end to them, but the mischief was done, and solely due to the success of the tanks we have suffered enormous losses ... ❜ (**E**)

C Allied tanks after the capture of Meaulte

The Germans were hit by the news of defeats for their friends. Greece had taken sides against Germany and Allied armies there could now advance. By 25 September, Bulgaria asked for peace. In Palestine, Turkish forces were retreating from the Arabs and the British. In Italy the last Austrian army lost to the British and Italians.

The Germans retreated to a specially constructed area of defences known as the Hindenburg Line. Concrete bunkers were arranged so that the whole area could be swept by machine-gun fire, and there were as many as eight or nine belts of barbed wire in front of the trenches.

The German government was changed, and the new chancellor, Prince Max of Baden approached America with an offer of peace. These negotiations broke down after two passenger ships were sunk by U-boats. The Germans could not fight for much longer. Their situation is summed up in a letter from Commander in Chief Hindenburg to Prince Max:

❛ *The supreme command demands an immediate despatch of a peace offer to our enemies. There no longer exists any hoping of forcing peace on our enemies. The enemy can bring in new and fresh reserves. The German army holds fast and repulses all attacks with success. But we must stop fighting to save the German people further useless sacrifices.* ❜ (**F**)

A member of the government wrote in October 1918:

❛ *We have no meat, potatoes cannot be delivered because we are short of 4000 trucks a day. Fat is unobtainable. The shortage is so great it is a mystery to me what the people of Berlin live on. The workers say 'Better a horrible end than an endless horror'.* ❜ (**G**)

To add to the miseries of the civilian population, influenza was sweeping the country. In the port of Kiel, 40 000 sailors mutinied. Germany's allies, Austria and Turkey, signed ceasefire agreements, and General Ludendorff was dismissed.

Then on 9 November 1918, Kaiser Wilhelm II abdicated and fled for safety to Holland, leaving the government in charge. Representatives were sent to Marshal Foch, and they met in a railway carriage (**H**). When asked what his terms for peace were, Foch replied that he had none. The Germans conceded that they could not fight on. 'Then', said Foch, 'you have come to surrender'.

The terms for armistice (ceasefire) were read and agreed, and the First World War ended at eleven o'clock on the eleventh day of the eleventh month of 1918.

The Germans were bitter about their defeat. A future leader, Adolf Hitler, said:

❛ *So it had all been in vain. In vain the sacrifices and privations . . . in vain the deaths of two millions . . . Had*

H   The meeting in a railway carriage at Compiègne, which ended the war

they died for this? So that a gang of wretched criminals could lay their hands on the fatherland? ❜ (**J**)

There was a search for somebody to blame. Hindenburg said, a week or so after the armistice:

❛ *In spite of the superiority of the enemy in men and materials, we could have brought the struggle to a favourable conclusion if determined and unanimous co-operation had existed between the army and those at home. The German army was stabbed in the back. It is plain enough on whom the blame lies.* ❜ (**K**)

??????????????????

1 In what way do we mark the 1918 armistice today?

2 Can **B** be accepted as a reliable and balanced source of information?

3 When Foch said that he had no terms for peace, what did he mean?

4 Why should tanks have such an unnerving effect on German soldiers, as described in **E**?

5 Why should Hindenburg feel that the German army had been 'stabbed in the back' (**K**)?

6 What are the contradictions between Hindenburg's accounts in **F** and **K**? Can you explain the differences?

20 'Make Germany Pay'

Representatives of the victorious Allies met at Versailles, outside Paris, on 18 January 1919. Their task was to redraw the map of Europe. They had to work fast, because the old empires of Europe were in ruins and people were suffering great hardship from poverty and hunger (**A**). They wanted peace. There was general agreement that the Great War was to be 'the war to end all wars'.

Each of the four representatives (photograph **B**) had his own ideas about what should happen. President Wilson (USA) proposed fourteen points for peace:

1 No more secret treaties.
2 The seas to be free to merchant ships at all times.
3 No restrictions on trade between countries.
4 Countries to reduce their armaments.
5 All claims to colonies to be treated in the interests of the people living there.
6 Russia to be free to choose her own system of government.
7 Belgium to be evacuated (freed of enemy presence).
8 Alsace-Lorraine to go back to France.
9 Italy's frontiers to be redrawn on the basis of nationality.
10 The peoples of the Austro-Hungarian Empire to be free.
11 The peoples in the Balkans should be free to form their own countries.
12 The peoples in the Turkish Empire should be free to form their own countries.
13 Poland to be 'recreated' and given access to the sea.
14 A League of Nations should be set up.

Wilson believed that the key to peace was a new organisation, The League of Nations. Wilson insisted that the articles of covenant (the rules) of the League should be written into each of the peace treaties. Source **C** is some extracts from the rules. You should be able to work out why Wilson believed that his League could stop future wars.

❝ *To promote international peace and achieve international peace and security; to accept the obligation not to resort to war.*

Members agree that when a dispute arises between them they shall submit the whole matter to arbitration.

Should any member resort to war, it shall be deemed to have committed an act of war against all members of the League. ❞ (**C**)

A A street kitchen in Cologne: here it was possible to obtain a meal of mutton and potatoes for twenty pfennig (about 1p)

B The Versailles Peace Conference, 1919: (*from left to right*) Lloyd George (Britain), Orlando (Italy), Clemenceau (France) and Wilson (USA)

The League of Nations was extremely important to President Wilson. Some of his colleagues considered that he was pushing the idea too hard. In the words of an American diplomat:

The President's obsession to a League blinds him to everything else. An immediate peace is nothing to him compared to the adoption of his covenant. The whole world wants peace. The President wants his League! I think the world will have to wait. (**D**)

The Germans were hopeful that the other countries would accept Wilson's fourteen points. They thought they would lead to a just and fair peace. In Britain, Lloyd George gave his view to parliament on the day after armistice:

We must not let any sense of revenge, any spirit of greed, any grasping desire override the fundamental principles of righteousness. The mandate of this government at the next election will mean that the British Government . . . will be in favour of a just peace. (**E**)

In the end, Germany was to be disappointed. Too many people wanted revenge. Sir Edward Geddes, MP, made this quite clear:

Germany is going to pay. I personally have no doubt that we are going to get everything out of her that you can squeeze out of a lemon and a bit more. Not only all the gold Germany has got but all her silver and jewels shall be handed over. All her pictures and libraries shall be sold to the allies and the proceeds used to pay the indemnity (the debt for the war). I would strip Germany as she stripped Belgium. (**F**)

France wanted to weaken Germany, to prevent it starting another war. This could be done by taking away the areas of land that were rich in mineral resources. France also wanted to disband the German navy.

Few people spoke up for Germany in 1919. Lloyd George tried hard to persuade his fellow MPs against seeking revenge, and to make a fair settlement, but the task was impossible. His words at the Versailles meeting were:

It will be . . . difficult for me . . . to disperse the illusions of the public . . . Four hundred MPs of the British Parliament have sworn to extract the last farthing from Germany that is owing to us. I will have to face up to them. But our duty is to act in the best interests of our countries . . . I am convinced Germany will not sign the sort of thing people are suggesting . . . Europe will remain mobilised (ready for war), our industries stopped, our treasuries bankrupt. (**G**)

Of all countries, France was most keen on punishing Germany. The French representative, Clemenceau, explained his right (in his opinion) to have a greater say than President Wilson:

America did not experience the first three years of war. In that time we lost three and a half million men. Our experiences have created in this country a strong demand for compensation. (**H**)

There was no alternative but to treat Germany harshly – the people of Britain and France were demanding it, on the grounds that Germany had started the war and should suffer for it. Feelings ran high, as this newspaper article (**J**) shows:

HAND HIM OVER!

The Kaiser is in Holland. More than a hundred years ago Napoleon was in Elba. From Elba Napoleon came forth relighting the fires of destruction, troubling all Europe again, till he and all his mischief were extinguished at Waterloo. The moral is plain. It is our business to call upon the Dutch Government to surrender the troubler of the world into our keeping, and with him any other of the brood who are now or may be hereafter in their territories. We must run no risks. We cannot afford to have the earth-fire that we have extinguished with our agony kindled anew. A million British lives have been spilt in the terrible struggle. They did not grudge the sacrifice, those men who died for us. But the awful offering is finished; it must not begin again. The Kaiser and his tribe must be brought to judgement and at least held in safe keeping, lest the whole world perish.

J A newspaper article demanding revenge on Germany

???????????????????

1 Wilson believed in self-determination – the right of peoples to form their own government. Which of his fourteen points bears this out?

2 What could have been in the back of Lloyd George's mind when he urged fair treatment for Germany?

3 What principle did each of the fourteen points stand for (freedom, equality, self-determination, peace, free trade and so on)? Consider each point.

4 Write two short speeches, one in favour of and one against punishing Germany.

5 Can you think of two powers which were not represented at Versailles, even though they were concerned in the war? Why were they absent?

21 Decision-making at Versailles

The class should divide into three delegations – American, British and French. Each delegation should use the ideas from page 40 to work out their proposed decision on each of the points below. Remember to argue from the point of view of each country. Once each delegation has worked out its proposals, the whole class should discuss each issue and then vote on it. (The actual decisions taken at Versailles are given on the next page).

Decision 1 Will you make Germany guilty of starting the war? If so, why?

Decision 2 What do you propose to do with the Kaiser (in exile in Holland)?

Decision 3 Germany's armed forces – will you limit them? If so, how? Think of men and equipment.

Decision 4 Germany's colonies – should she lose them? Why? Who can look after them? South Africa wants South-west Africa, New Zealand wants Samoa; Australia, New Guinea. Could the League of Nations help?

Decision 5 Should Germany pay for the war? (These payments are called *reparations*.) If so, how much? If you cannot fix a sum, you could set a commission to work out a fair amount. See sources **A** and **B**.

From Colonel House's diary (an American):

❛ *The British now put in a tentative demand on Germany of 120 billion dollars and the French think Germany should pay 200 billion dollars. In other words the French want the Germans to pay 200 times what the French paid in 1871 which the French then thought excessive. Our people think the maximum it can be is 22 billion dollars.* ❜ (**A**)

Lloyd George:

❛ *I see great advantages in not declaring today a figure representing the total that Germany owes. Whatever figure we decide upon, many people in England and France will shout 'It's too little'.* ❜ (**B**)

Decision 6 Austria is now a small country with a German-speaking people. They may wish to join Germany. Can you stop this happening?

C

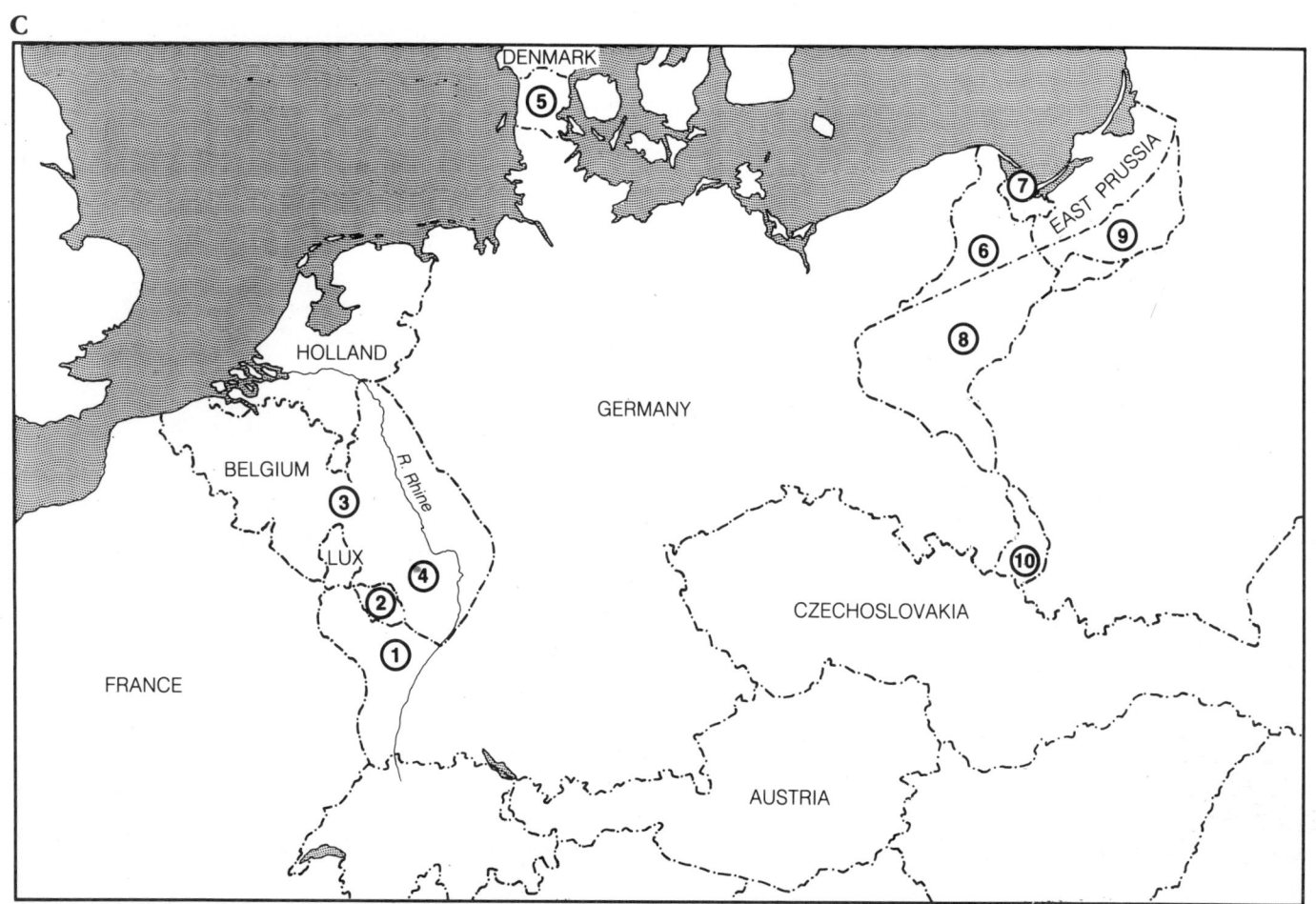

Germany and her frontiers

Find each of the areas below on map **C.** Consider the point of view of your country and any extra information, and select which proposal you would support. Give reasons for your choice. For those marked ** you could work out a more complicated proposal involving the League of Nations. You can select a plebiscite or referendum of the people. This would mean asking the people who lived there what they wanted.

Alsace-Lorraine (*Area* **1**)

Had been French until 1870. An important industrial area.

   i Germany to retain
   ii Give to France

Saar (*Area* **2**)

Very important coalfield. Population is German.

   i Germany to retain
   ii Give to France
   iii **

Eupen/Malmedy (*Area* **3**)

An area with coal and iron. Belgium was neutral in 1914 and suffered heavily when Germany attacked her.

   i Germany to retain
   ii Give to Belgium

The Rhineland (*Area* **4**)

Clemenceau: *He did not believe in the principle of self determination which allowed a man to clutch at your throat the first time it was convenient to him . . . and would not consent to any time limit being placed on the separation of the Rhineland from the rest of Germany . . . Alone against Germany, invaded and bleeding. We do not ask for territory but for guarantees. Those offered us at present – disarmament, League of Nations, are inadequate. It is essential that the left bank of the Rhine be closed to the political and military schemes of Germany.*

Lloyd George: *To compel Germany to accept the occupation of the Rhineland indefinitely would provoke fresh tension, even war in Europe . . . the occupation of German land should be limited and come to an end in a reasonable time.*

   i Germany to retain
   ii Give to France
   iii Create a new country to act as a 'buffer' between France and Germany
   iv **

Schleswig (*Area* **5**)

Has been German since the 1860s. Two halves: the South has more Germans, the North more Danes.

   i Germany to retain
   ii Give to Denmark

   iii Split them North to Denmark; South to Germany.
   iv Have a plebiscite.

West Prussia (*Area* **6**)

German speaking. Essential for Poland to give her access to the sea, but this would split off East Prussia from the rest of Germany.

   i Germany to retain
   ii Give to Poland
   iii **

Lloyd George: *agreed that it was hardly possible to draw any line that would not have Germans on both sides of it, but he thought it was dangerous to assign two million Germans to Poland. This was a considerable population not less than that of Alsace-Lorraine.*

Clemenceau stated: *there was a need for a strong Poland. President Wilson had assumed in his fourteen points a newly created Poland. The League of Nations was a fine creation, but it could not be made without nations. As one of the nations concerned, Poland was most necessary as a buffer on the East as France formed a buffer on the West.*

Danzig (*Area* **7**)

German population. Chief port on the Baltic. Would be very important for Poland.

   i Germany to retain
   ii Give to Poland
   iii **

Posen and Thorn (*Area* **8**)

Similar comments as for *6*.

   i Germany to retain
   ii Give to Poland

Allenstein/Marienwerder (*Area* **9**)

Not necessary for the 'Polish corridor' – see *6*. Population mixed German and Polish.

   i Germany to retain
   ii Poland to gain
   iii Plebiscite

Silesia (*Area* **10**)

All points as for *9* – but note this area has good mineral resources.

   i Germany to retain
   ii Poland to gain
   iii Plebiscite

22 Versailles: the Results

The representatives of the Allies at Versailles declared Germany guilty of starting the war and accountable for its results. It was decided to bring the Kaiser to trial, but Holland, where he fled just before the end of the war, refused to let him go.

Germany was to be allowed an army, limited to 100 000 men, but could not have tanks, warplanes or submarines. Its colonies were to be taken over by the League of Nations. Former German territories in Europe were to be taken away (**J**), and either returned to the countries from which they were taken in the first place or handed over to other governments. Union with Austria was forbidden.

Repayment for war damage and loss was to be made, the amount to be fixed at a later date.

These were the peace terms that Germany had to accept. There was no choice – the country was in no position to start fighting again. The signing was carried out with ceremony:

❢ There is a hush followed by a military order. The guards flash their swords with a loud click. 'Make the Germans enter', says Clemenceau. Two hussars march in in single file. Isolated and pitiable come the two German delegates. The silence is terrifying. They keep their eyes away from the two thousand staring eyes, fixed on the ceiling. They are deathly pale. Clemenceau says a few words. The Germans leap up when he has finished since they know they are first to sign. They are motioned to sit down again . . . They sign . . . Suddenly from outside the crash of guns thundered a salute. We kept our seats whilst the Germans were conducted away like prisoners from the dock, their eyes fixed on some distant point. ❢ (**A**)

Britain considered that the cause of peace would be helped if the German navy was handed over. Accordingly, the fleet was sailed to Scapa Flow, off north-east Scotland, and scuttled (deliberately sunk). The cartoon **B** is a comment on the event, and recalls a famous signal made by Admiral Nelson at the sea battle of Trafalgar 114 years before: 'England expects that every man this day will do his duty'.

The amount of compensation to be paid was fixed by the Reparations Committee in 1921 at £6600 million. The

B　A cartoon commenting on the sinking of the German fleet at Scapa Flow

THE END OF A PERFECT "TAG."

C　A British view of the German government's protest over compensation payments

THE RECKONING.

PAN-GERMAN. "MONSTROUS, I CALL IT. WHY, IT'S FULLY A QUARTER OF WHAT *WE* SHOULD HAVE MADE *THEM* PAY, IF WE'D WON."

"PERHAPS IT WOULD GEE-UP BETTER IF WE LET IT TOUCH EARTH"

D A British cartoon opposing the 'make Germany pay' policy

German government was staggered by this huge amount and protested strongly. Work out what **C** is trying to say about these protests. Not all Britons felt the same way, however (cartoon **D**). J.M. Keynes, Britain's financial adviser at Versailles, wrote a book called *The Economic Consequences of the Peace,* in which he argued that it was impossible for Germany to pay such a large amount. Keynes's book sold by the million and was translated into eleven languages. Later critics have disagreed with him, pointing out that Germany spent more than £6600 million when rebuilding its armed forces in the 1930s.

Winston Churchill's opinion was:

❛ *The economic clauses were malignant and silly to an extent that made them futile. Germany was condemned to pay reparations on a fabulous scale. People failed to understand that no defeated country can pay a tribute on a scale which would meet the cost of modern war. Few voices were raised to explain that reparations can only be paid in services or goods and that when these goods arrive in the demanding countries they hit local industries.* ❜ (**E**)

Churchill could understand that sales of German goods in Britain would damage British markets.

President Wilson was most disappointed by the treaty. When he went back to the United States, he found that the American Congress refused to accept the peace treaty and the League of Nations. In despair, he toured the states. He failed to win over the American people, and the League of Nations was seriously weakened because the USA did not join. Wilson said:

❛ *If America does not join the League I can predict with absolute certainty that within a generation there will be another war.* ❜ (**F**)

Germany was in a bitter mood, and it was not long before the threat of war hung over Europe once again. The thirst for revenge for the humiliation of Versailles was stirred up by speeches and articles like this one from the *Deutsche Zeitung* newspaper:

❛ *Vengeance! German Nation*
Today in the Hall of Mirrors of Versailles the disgraceful Treaty is being signed. Do not forget it! The German people will with unceasing labour press forward to reconquer the place among nations to which it is entitled. Then will come the vengeance for the shame of 1919. ❜ (**G**)

Adolf Hitler, who had served in the army and was becoming politically active, was clear in his view:

❛ *Only fools, liars and criminals could hope for mercy from the enemy. In these nights hatred grew in me, hatred for those responsible for the dead.* ❜ (**H**)

J Decision-making at Versailles: the Results (see p 42)

> **Alsace-Lorraine** (*Area* **1**) Given to France.
>
> **Saar** (*Area* **2**) League of Nations to control. France to receive coal for fifteen years. Then a plebiscite.
>
> **Eupen/Malmedy** (*Area* **3**) Given to Belgium.
>
> **The Rhineland** (*Area* **4**) Germany to retain, but as a de-militarized zone.
>
> **Schleswig** (*Area* **5**) Plebiscite.
>
> **West Prussia** (*Area* **6**) Given to Poland.
>
> **Danzig** (*Area* **7**) League of Nations to control.
>
> **Posen and Thorn** (*Area* **8**) Given to Poland.
>
> **Allenstein/Marienwerder** (*Area* **9**) Plebiscite.
>
> **Silesia** (*Area* **10**) Plebiscite.

?????????????????

1 What parts of **A** give the impression that the German delegates were treated like criminals?

2 Would the cartoonist who drew **C** agree with Keynes? What about the artist responsible for **D**?

3 Germany fell behind with her reparations (repayments) in 1923. Write a letter from the German to the French government explaining why this happened.

4 List the ways in which the Treaty of Versailles might lead to another war, and discuss whether the treaty was the best that could have been achieved.

5 Which pieces of evidence suggest that Germany will eventually try to overthrow the treaty?

23 The Break-up of Empires

By the time the peace meeting took place at Versailles in 1919 the great Austro-Hungarian Empire, which had dominated Europe, was shattered. Governments had been formed to run the new countries of Czechoslovakia and Yugoslavia; and Italy, Poland and Rumania had gained new territories. In preparing the boundaries of the new countries, which were formed by joining older, smaller countries, President Wilson considered that language was important. He was right up to a point, but did not allow for the fact that several languages might be spoken in one country, or that one language might be spoken in several countries. The best frontier may not be the one laid down by language – a country needs good defences, industrial opportunities and transport links. All these influence where a frontier should run.

The Sudetenland contained three million Germans – should it be given back to Germany, or to Czechoslovakia, by Wilson's rule? Czechoslovakia itself was worried. Germany was closed in to the west, and might at some future time seek outlets through the south and east (in other words, through Czechoslovakia). The Czech negotiator at Versailles said:

' The German mass, now eighty millions, could not push west, its way was blocked by the developed nations. It would seek outlets south and east. The Czech frontiers are especially important. They must be drawn through the Bohemian mountain chain. ' **(A)**

It was felt that the Bohemian mountains would form a natural defensive barrier.

Italy had assisted in the war, and promises of territory had been made by the Allies in 1915. The territory included Dalmatia, which Yugoslavia claimed. There was no doubt that Dalmatia had been promised to Italy, and the Allies were faced with a dilemma: should they honour the promise? In the light of experience, it was felt that it might be best not to do so. The British cabinet announced:

' The British war cabinet desire to point out to the Italian government that the allocation of large areas of the Ottoman (Turkish) Empire to Italy can hardly be justified by the effort hitherto made by Italy in the war as compared with the sacrifices already made by Great Britain, France and Russia. ' **(B)**

President Wilson rejected Italy's claim with these words:

' I feel myself obliged to adapt every conclusion at which I arrived as closely to the fourteen points as possible . . .

D The Break-up of the Austro-Hungarian Empire

—— Frontier of Austria–Hungary 1914
–·–·– National frontiers 1919

E Mandates formed from the Turkish Empire

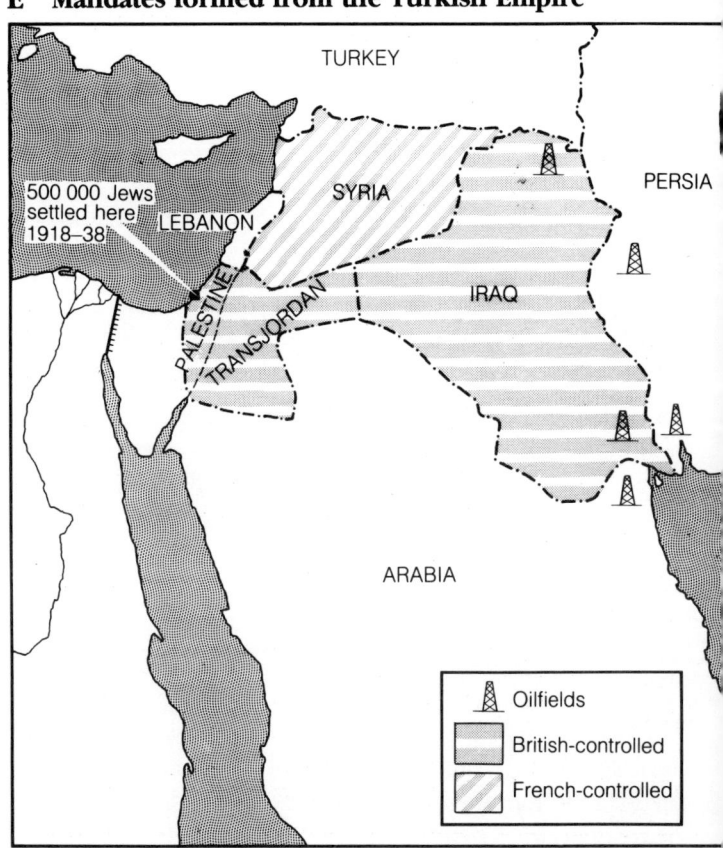

⚓ Oilfields
British-controlled
French-controlled